How to Get into Politics— and Why

A Reader

by Michael Dukakis and Paul Simon

EDUCATION GROUP
A Houghton Mifflin Company

AUTHORS | **Michael Dukakis**

After beginning in politics at the local level and then moving into the state legislature, Michael Dukakis became governor of Massachusetts and eventually ran, in 1988, for the Democratic nomination for the presidency. He now teaches at Northeastern University in Boston and at UCLA in Los Angeles.

Paul Simon

Rising from the position of editor of the newspaper in the small town of Troy, Illinois, Paul Simon went on to serve fourteen years in the Illinois State Legislature, 10 years in the U.S. House of Representatives, and twelve years as U.S. Senator. He now heads the Public Policy Institute at Southern Illinois University in Carbondale, Illinois.

DESIGN | **Ovresat Paredes**

Printed in the United States of America

International Standard Book Number: 0-669-046796-0

1 2 3 4 5 6 7 8 9—P00— 08 07 06 05 04 03 02 01 00

Contents

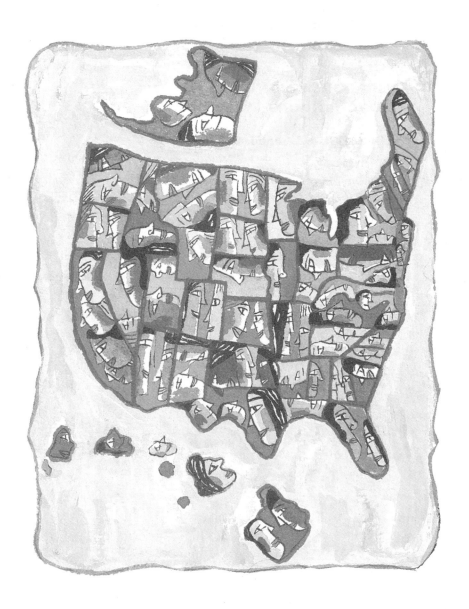

Introduction

E ver since both of us got into politics, we've been asked again and again why we ever took the plunge.

People particularly want to know how difficult it is; whether or not it is possible to have a decent family life and be a politician; how intrusive the press is; how we cope with all the pressure.

What motivates people to get into politics?

This book attempts to answer this question in two ways. First, it tackles the subject directly by outlining a plan to get into politics—how to start, how to pick a party, announce and file petitions, and even campaign. Second, it presents the personal political narratives of distinguished men and women who, like us, have served their country in positions great and small—from Supreme Court Justice to the local city council. These stories tell how—and why—they took the plunge into politics in the hopes that you, too, may someday follow us.

To start, we thought we'd begin by telling our own stories, so that you might see right at the beginning how and why we got into politics. Our stories illustrate, we think, that you do not need a great deal of money or friends in high places, only a will and desire to make a difference.

We hope you'll find a reason here to get involved, whether it's in your school, place of worship, or town. Perhaps it will be, as it was for us, the experience of your life.

 Personal Political Narratives

A Fulfilling Life

MICHAEL DUKAKIS

I can't remember a time when I wasn't interested in politics.

In fact, I clearly remember the presidential campaign of 1940 when I was seven and Franklin Delano Roosevelt and Wendell Wilkie were running for the presidency. My brother, who was three years older than I was, and I set up a card table in the middle of our living room; drew up a chart with the names of the then 48 states on it and columns in which to record the convention delegate vote; and sat attentively listening to the radio (this was in the pre-television days) and recording the votes as they came in on the various ballots. While FDR was renominated easily for what was then a very controversial third term, the Republican nomination fight was a spirited one, and Wilkie had to beat both Governor Dewey of New York and Senator Taft of Ohio to win it.

What was a seven-year-old boy doing taking down convention votes? That's a good question. I suspect part of it had to do with my Greek heritage. Both of my parents were immigrants. Neither was a political activist. But Greeks have a long and proud political tradition. Every Greek-American child knows from an early age that Athens was the birthplace of democracy. Politics—and especially Greek politics—is a hot topic around Greek immigrant dinner tables.

Beyond that, however, my parents never let my brother and me forget that this country had welcomed them and their families in the early 1900s; had given them a chance to get an education which almost certainly would have been denied them in Greece and western Turkey from which they had come; and had opened up a world of opportunity to them that was uniquely

American. My dad became the first American-trained, Greek-speaking doctor in metropolitan Boston. My mother was one of the first young Greek immigrant women ever to go to college, and she became a schoolteacher.

Under the circumstances, we first-generation Americans understood that we had a special responsibility to make our own contribution to the common weal. "Much has been given to you, and much is expected of you." If I heard it once, I heard it a thousand times.

So when my third-grade class decided to have an election for class president, I ran and won; and, at least until 1990, I've been running ever since. In fact, it is no surprise that many people who enter political life do so first by getting actively involved in school politics. I certainly was in high school and college, and I know many of my colleagues in government were also. Why? Because school politics gave us a chance to change things for the better, and we had a real commitment to doing so.

Once I returned from military service in Korea to go to law school in the Boston area, it seemed the natural and logical thing to get actively involved in local politics. Furthermore, John F. Kennedy, who represented my state in the U.S. Senate, was just beginning to get his campaign for the presidency together, and he was an enormously inspiring force in the lives of many of us who were growing up politically in the late 1950s.

There was one other strong force behind my desire to run for political office. Massachusetts, unfortunately, was one of the most corrupt states in the country in the 1950s and early 1960s. A state that had produced some of the nation's greatest statesmen and the exciting young President that was elected in 1960 had a terrible reputation for some of the shabbiest politics in America. A lot of us decided that we had to do something about it, and it was certainly a big motivating force in my decision to run for public office.

CONTINUED

A Fulfilling Life CONTINUED

I started at a very low level in local politics and slowly worked my way up to the state legislature and, ultimately, to my state's governorship and my party's nomination for the presidency. Others may choose a different route. Personally, I felt that I was a far better public servant because of the experience I had had both campaigning and serving in local office. It is not an absolute requirement for distinguished service in politics, but it sure helps.

I've never regretted the decision to plunge into the politics of my community, state, and country. I've had an incredible life—an immigrant's son who served for almost 12 years as the highest officeholder in his state and almost made it to the White House. In what country other than the United States would that be possible? In short, I've had the opportunity that politics gives one to try to make a real difference in the lives of one's fellow citizens and the world in which we, and they, live.

I can't think of a life more fulfilling and satisfying than that, and these days I spend a lot of my time as a professor at Northeastern University in Boston and UCLA in Los Angeles trying to encourage and inspire young people to follow the same path.

Personal Political Narratives

If You Believe in Something

PAUL SIMON

My father, a Lutheran minister, did not involve himself in partisan politics, but I remember him taking me at the age of eight to a speech by Eleanor Roosevelt, the wife of President Franklin D. Roosevelt. My father also served on the board of our rural school district in Oregon where we had several grades to a room. So I grew up in a family that paid attention to public issues.

Of long-range significance to me was when the President ordered 115,000 Japanese Americans from their homes in California, Oregon, and Washington—not one of whom had committed a crime—and told them they had one to three days to sell all they owned and put their belongings into one suitcase, and they would be taken off to camps. My father objected in comments for a local radio station. This was three months after the bombing of Pearl Harbor by the Japanese, and patriotic fervor in our country had reached extremes. Thirteen years old at the time, I was embarrassed by the comments of my friends, portraying my father as an unpatriotic citizen. Years later I came to appreciate how right and courageous my father had been, and I wondered where the other people were who should have stood up for the rights of their fellow Americans. This experience taught me a lesson I have never forgotten: If you believe in something, have the courage to stand up for it.

As a youth who read newspapers avidly, I came to appreciate the most widely read political columnist in the nation, Walter Lippmann. People in high public office read him and listened to him. He influenced national and international policy. I wanted to become another Walter Lippmann.

CONTINUED

If You Believe in Something CONTINUED

At the end of my junior year in college, I had the chance to become publisher of a small weekly newspaper in Troy, Illinois. This was my opportunity! I wrote commentaries on national issues that I felt would gain me recognition beyond my immediate readership—but much to my dismay the world seemed neither startled nor interested in what I had to say. A few newspapers would reprint or comment on my observations, but the anticipated avalanche of recognition did not develop.

What did develop at my doorstep was clear evidence that the sheriff and prosecuting attorney of the county in which I lived and published the newspaper were cooperating with underworld criminal elements. My small newspaper started writing about this, accumulating evidence, and soon I had Governor Adlai Stevenson and a few national figures paying attention to the blatant abuse of power in our Illinois county. Television had just begun to reach into every neighborhood in the nation. Senator Estes Kefauver of Tennessee, who chaired televised hearings on the tie between politics and organized crime, called on me as a witness. That greatly raised my visibility. I had been trying to get honest candidates to run for sheriff and prosecuting attorney. People feared doing it. I did not want to become a sheriff and I am not a lawyer, so I could not become the prosecuting attorney. So I finally ran for state representative and, at the age of 25, surprised everyone—including myself—by winning.

I served 14 years in the state legislature, four as lieutenant governor— ran for governor and narrowly lost—and then served for 10 years in the U.S. House and 12 years in the U.S. Senate. In 1988, I sought the Democratic nomination for the presidency, but an outstanding governor from Massachusetts, Michael Dukakis, bested me in that effort.

My years in public life have been intensely rewarding. I am grateful to the people who gave me the opportunity to serve.

After 22 years in Washington, I voluntarily retired and am now teaching at Southern Illinois University in Carbondale, where I head the Public Policy Institute—and I'm doing a great deal of voluntary work, both within our nation and internationally.

To young people who look for a powerful combination of public service, personal satisfaction, and pleasure, I recommend the political life.

1 | **Why Get into Politics?**

hat motivates people to get into politics?

In our experience, and we have served with literally thousands of dedicated public servants, it is usually because they are not satisfied with the status quo and believe that by getting actively involved in the political life of their community or state or country, they can make a real difference—not just for themselves but for their fellow citizens.

You may ask, "Are Paul Simon and Mike Dukakis really that idealistic?" While we both would like to think we had, and have, high ideals, we are hardly alone. In the pages of this book, you will meet a number of people, men and women, often from poor or average economic backgrounds, who have achieved much in public life. Some are Republicans; some are Democrats. Some are conservative, and some are liberal. We know them all, and they are all motivated by a desire to make this a better world.

Few of them started their political careers with famous names, although some did. Most grew up in homes where important issues were discussed and debated, but few came from political families. Almost none were born to wealth. Yet every one of them has succeeded in politics, and whether still active or semi-retired from elective office, they, like the two of us, can look back on things they have done that give them an enormous amount of personal fulfillment and satisfaction.

We believe that there is an instinct in almost all of us that wants to give something back to the community and country that has given us

so much. In each of us, there is something of the noble and something of the beast, and political leaders can appeal to the noble or the beast. An extreme example, Hitler, appealed to the worst in people. Abraham Lincoln appealed to the best in us. The sense that we should give something back to the community and country that have done so much for us can be appealed to and bring about positive change. But you need to be properly motivated. For Michael Dukakis, the immigrant background of his parents and their love of their adopted country played an enormous role in his sense of obligation and service. For Paul Simon, the son of a Lutheran minister, it was the sense inculcated in him from birth that we are on this planet to serve others. The other contributors to this book have described, in their own words, their personal political stories.

Often a local issue got them involved. For Mario Cuomo, the son of Italian immigrants who literally lived in the back of his parents' little store in Queens, New York, a series of local controversies came to him as a young lawyer before he even thought of running for office. Steve Goldsmith had a growing concern about the rising crime rate in his native Indianapolis. A teacher inspired Supreme Court Justice Sandra Day O'Connor to enter public service as a young prosecutor and eventually run for office. Unhappiness about their children's schools or a local environmental problem that cries out for solutions or anger at the injustice of something that has happened in a community provokes people to get involved and want to do something.

And there is nothing wrong with being fascinated by the game of politics, a game that has winners and losers but is vastly more important than if the Boston Red Sox or the St. Louis Cardinals win. For us, local and state corruption brought us into politics. Each of us lived in a state with great strengths but with a reputation for sleazy politics and outright graft and corruption. John Kennedy had just been elected President of the United States—young, gifted, a constant source of inspiration to young people such as us. Why, we reasoned, couldn't our states provide the same kind of leadership at the state level that Jack Kennedy was providing for the nation? And what, more importantly, would we do about it? Michael Dukakis, a young lawyer, joined a small band of like-minded colleagues in the Massachusetts legislature, determined to clean up the incompetence and corruption that they saw around them and try, as best they could, to give their state the same kind of inspired leadership that President Kennedy, a native son of Massachusetts, gave the country until a gunman tragically cut his life short. Paul Simon started as a crusading local editor who decided that he would take the fight right into his state legislature.

I s there a trace of arrogance in this? Who were we, after all, to think that we could make a difference where others had failed?

Maybe we were a little cocky, but that is the beauty of the American political system. It is the most open in the world. You don't need a ticket of admission. You don't need a famous name. You certainly don't need a lot of personal wealth, as we both can testify.

What you do need is self-confidence and a healthy ego, because you will be challenged on more than one occasion. You need an understanding family, but making sure your family comes first in your life is a challenge for all Americans these days. And you have to believe deeply in your cause and in your ability to make a difference. Politics is not for the faint-hearted.

Even those who decide not to participate—or even vote—are in a real sense "participating" by turning the decision making over to others. Martin Luther King's famous letter from a Birmingham jail condemned those who by their non-involvement permitted an unjust and inhumane policy of rigid segregation to continue. In Germany, people who were nonparticipants permitted an evil dictator, Adolf Hitler, to come to power. He did not need their support; he only needed their silence.

As you read this, you may already be involved in politics. Some of you are active in student government. Why? Probably in part because you have seen things in your school that bother you, and you want to make them better.

Many of you are involved in community service, either through your school—and more and more schools are requiring public service—or through your church or synagogue or mosque. Others of you may in a special way be making contributions to the betterment of your community. Whether you know it or not, that means you have taken your first small step into political life.

Why have you decided to devote time to helping people at the senior center in your town, or mentor a boy or girl who is struggling in middle school, or become an active member of a drug and alcohol peer counseling group? For the same reason that the people you are going to meet in this book have entered politics. You recognize—as they do—that by working together we can make a real difference in our communities and state and country, and a major way to do that is to get involved in public life.

The United States has millions of people who are doing exactly what you are doing—getting involved. What too many people are not doing, however, is thinking seriously about getting active in political life—and that's what we hope this book will encourage you to do.

B oth of us are continually asked two questions when we speak on high school and college campuses: Why did you get into politics? If someone is interested, how does he or she get involved? This book is an attempt to answer those questions.

One of the first things you will probably want to know is how someone in politics puts up with the criticism and pressure and even, occasionally, the personal abuse that seems to be growing with the explosion in tabloid television, attack advertising, and what seems to be a more intensely partisan political atmosphere. Every day we meet people who ask us if we aren't relieved to be out of active politics.

Both of us react the same way to that kind of question. Happy to be out of it? Relieved of pressure? We loved our careers in politics. We enjoyed the pressure. Why? Because people who go into politics usually relish the opportunity to tackle tough issues; to build coalitions, often with people with whom you don't often agree; to see how our efforts impact favorably on the lives of others. This work is not limited to legislative debates or official actions. Each of us and the people you are going to meet in this book have been able to help countless numbers of citizens who called on us for help: the deserving student who needed scholarship assistance to go to college; the immigrant family that needed help in navigating the bureaucratic complications of the Immigration and Naturalization Service; the community group trying to stop some government agency from bulldozing their homes when there were other and better alternatives; the working family without health insurance that asked for a helping hand in getting the medical care they needed.

That, too, is an important part of politics and public service: helping ordinary citizens to get the services that their government is supposed to be providing them.

A career in politics won't all be "peaches and cream." There will be frustrations and turns in the road that may not be happy ones. We represent the combined experience of more than 60 years in active political life. We have tasted victory and defeat. You can take it from us: winning is better than losing.

B ut nothing—nothing—matches the personal fulfillment and satisfaction that comes from being actively involved in the political life of your community, state, and country.

Furthermore, it is fun—most of the time. You will meet some of the best people you have ever met, because they too got into politics because they wanted to "do good." You will have a million laughs. You may even meet your life's partner. Paul did. He and his late wife Jeanne met when they were both members of the Illinois legislature, and they were husband and wife for 39 years.

Kitty wasn't holding public office when Mike and she first began dating, but she had been a student leader in high school and college and an elected member of the student senate at Penn State University. Of course, Mike didn't take any chances. He decided to run for the Massachusetts legislature about six months after they started dating, and he wanted to make sure that the woman he loved could handle the

stresses and strains of political life. At the September primary in 1962, he asked her to campaign for him for 13 straight hours in front of one of the toughest polling places in his district. When he won that precinct by a decisive margin, he knew she was the woman for him!

Is politics intrusive? Will your family feel the sting of the public criticism that is leveled against you? Undoubtedly, and they will probably take it harder than you do.

But don't be put off by the idea that you can't live a good and decent life if you are active in politics. You can, and we hope we are living testimonials to that fact, despite the occasional difficulties that have come our way.

Is there any important pursuit in life not subject at some point to public exposure and public criticism? Mike has a first cousin who is one of the leading actresses in America, Olympia Dukakis. She has worked tirelessly for years to earn that reputation. So has her husband, Lou Zorich, a capable actor in his own right, and they have managed to raise three fine children. Yet every time Olympia or Lou goes on the stage or makes a movie, they and their fellow actors can be savaged by the critics and literally be put out of business.

Compared to that, politics is not bad. Particularly at this early point in your lives, with so many possibilities open to you who are just beginning to think about careers and what you want to do in life, this is a great time to explore politics and public service as a career. The seemingly endless conflict between the United States and what we used to call the Soviet Union that totally dominated both of our political lives is over. The American economy is thriving. Despite a number of regional conflicts that continue to plague our planet, this is the most peaceful world we've ever lived in. In fact, we'd love to be starting all over again.

But the future is up to you. We've written this book and invited some outstanding public servants to share their experiences with you, because we hope you will seize the torch and provide your communities and our world with the kind of courageous and farsighted leadership they need.

Go for it!

How and Why I Got into Politics

DICK ARMEY

My wife always reminds me, this career in politics is more than she bargained for.

In the early 1980s, I was a college professor, working 30–40 hours a week, getting home in time to take the kids to the pool. Who would give that up?

But I felt the pull of the Reagan revolution. For more than a decade, I'd been teaching free-market economics. I'd been watching as the world slowly turned from the Keyneslan economics of big government to a realization that markets work. First, Milton Friedman won the Nobel Prize in Economics in 1976—an enormous victory for free markets in the world of ideas. Then Ronald Reagan won the presidency on a platform of individual freedom and free markets. I finally saw what I believed in and what I'd been teaching getting put into practice.

I heartily cheered the new faces in Washington who were cutting taxes and spending and getting the country out of the stagflation of the 1970s. But I never thought it was a world I'd be part of—until I discovered C-SPAN. I sat watching one night, during what is called "special orders," when members of Congress deliver speeches after the legislative business for the day is over. These speeches weren't much different from the lectures I was giving in the college classroom. While I hope I was reaching the 30 or so students in each of my classes, here was an opportunity to reach America with the message that freedom works. One night in 1983 it just hit me—I turned to my wife and said, "I can do that." So I did.

It was an enormous change of lifestyle—commuting from Dallas to Washington, being away from my family, and working late nights. In exchange, I've been a part of a wonderful time in our nation's history. The nation over the last two decades has come to understand that markets work—that freedom works. I can only hope that I helped make that happen.

When I got to Washington in 1985, we had budget deficits as far as the eye could see. For every new dollar the government collected from the taxpayers, we were spending $1.59. Washington's appetite for spending seemed unstoppable.

I was determined to find some innovative ways to slow the growth in federal spending. I started making my mark quickly. In 1988, as only a second-term member of Congress, I wrote and passed legislation creating the Base Closure and Realignment Commission to close down unnecessary military bases around the country. I took what I had been teaching in my economics classes—public-choice theory, which emphasizes the role of incentives—and put it into practice. For too long, individual members of Congress had no incentives to close down an unnecessary military base. Certainly the member of Congress representing that base saw an immediate incentive to fight hard to keep it open and protect his or her constituents who worked there. And other members of Congress had the incentive to agree, so that the base in their district wouldn't be next.

The only way to get rid of unnecessary military bases was to change the incentives members of Congress faced. I changed the dynamics by creating a commission of military experts to get away from the politics and produce a list of unnecessary bases. The Congress had to accept the list—all or nothing—on an up or down vote. No member could approach the vote trying to save one base in his district. Instead, the package was big enough that

CONTINUED

everyone had the incentive to vote for it, and get public recognition for doing the right thing and ending unnecessary spending. Today, five rounds of base closings are saving the taxpayers about $4 billion per year.

As a back bencher in the minority party, I knew I wasn't going to have many of these legislative successes. I understood that to get the votes to pass bills that scaled back the size and scope of government, I first had to take my case to the public. I spent much of my time plotting floor amendments that would expose wasteful spending and doing television and radio interviews to highlight how much waste there was in government.

Many Republicans in Congress at the time didn't make the same effort to tell America what was going on here. They had grown used to being in the minority in Congress—never holding the chairmanships and never getting to set the agenda. But, in the early 1990s, it became very apparent that more and more Americans were beginning to share our agenda of smaller, less intrusive government. First, President Clinton cajoled the Congress into passing the largest tax increase in history—over the outraged cries of working Americans across the nation. Then, in the next year, the country made itself heard, and Congress defeated the President's government-run health care plan.

America had finally heard the message my fellow conservatives and I had been delivering for years. It was time to break out of our minority mindset and ask the nation to give us the levers of power in the Congress.

And so the Contract with America was born. Working with Newt Gingrich, I put together the Contract as the legislative agenda we would pursue if Republicans had a majority in Congress, including a balanced budget, welfare reform, a $500-per-child tax credit, national missile defense, an end to frivolous lawsuits, and a Congress that operated on a smaller budget.

Winning the majority was hard work. I was honored when my colleagues then asked me to take on the responsibilities of Majority Leader. We quickly went to work, keeping the promises made in the Contract. We changed America for the better.

We balanced the budget and cut family taxes. Today the federal budget is in surplus for the first time in a generation. The economy is booming, creating more and better paying jobs every day. We reformed the welfare system to reward work and responsibility. Today, teen pregnancy is down, and more than 3 million Americans have moved from welfare to work.

I'm proud to have been part of the changes that have again made America the land of opportunity and prosperity. And I look forward to the work we still have ahead of us, making our public schools once again the best in the world, further reducing the burden of big government, restoring America's national defense, and ensuring retirement security for current and future generations of senior citizens.

I think back to my days as a college professor, watching C-SPAN and thinking of politics as a vaguely interesting curiosity, and I can hardly believe I've been lucky enough to have had a hand in extending Ronald Reagan's morning in America.

Dick Armey, Majority Leader of the 105th and 106th Congresses, is a Republican from the 26th District located in Dallas, Texas.

To Make a Difference

WILLIE BROWN

I came of age at a time and in a place that systematically and legally excluded people of my racial stock from most of the rights and privileges of citizenship. We could neither vote nor hold office, serve on most juries, eat in most restaurants, stay in most hotels, travel freely on public transportation, attend the best colleges and universities, or marry outside our race.

Not surprisingly, a career in politics was not even on my radar screen when I packed my diploma from Mineola Colored High School and left my home in Texas to go to college in San Francisco. I only knew that somehow I wanted to make a difference.

That desire ultimately led me to law school. I knew lawyers could make a difference, even win against the most intractable problems, as Thurgood Marshall and his team had in *Brown vs. the Board of Education of Topeka, Kansas*. When I became a lawyer, San Francisco law firms were still politely uninterested in hiring black associates, so I hung out my shingle in my neighborhood. My early clients consisted of street hustlers, petty criminals, con artists, ladies of the evening and their handlers, plus a large category of folks in some sort of need. For these people—from an elderly woman served with an eviction notice, to a young mother in desperate need of child support from a deadbeat ex-husband, to a father of three, duped into paying usurious interest rates for a second-hand car—the judicial system almost always worked too slowly to help, even when the law was on their side. More often than I found conscionable, the law was emphatically not on their side.

Or always on mine, for that matter. Once I was established in my practice, my wife and I decided it was time to move our family into a bigger home. One morning, my wife and a friend were driving past a new residential development, when they decided to stop and look at a model home. When they entered the front door, the sales people literally ran out the back. They said they were closed for the day. In fact, they were simply determined not to show, never mind sell, one of their houses to an African American. My wife and I had scrimped and struggled to get me through law school. I was now a member in good standing of the California Bar, yet we still couldn't even tour one of these homes, because our skin was not the approved color.

I channeled my outrage into action—not in a courtroom, because the laws of that day offered no remedy—but by spearheading demonstrations against the developers and their agents. I had long ago realized the importance of politics and had been involved in various political organizations, issues, and causes, but this was a turning point for me. I understood—better than I ever had before—that my skills and my commitment as a lawyer were only as effective as the laws to which I could apply them. I came to believe that I could make a bigger difference as a lawmaker. So, in 1962, I ran for the State Assembly—and lost! I tried again in 1964 and won.

More important than the circumstances that led me into politics are the things that drove me to stay. Many good people don't. They get disillusioned, tired of the long hours, impatient with the slow pace of change, desirous of better pay, or fed up with the incivilities of their opponents and the press. Like most new legislators, I quickly (and rather brutally) learned that I was but one voice among many, that my very newness was itself a liability, and that accomplishing any of the things I wanted to accomplish would require mastering the rules, procedures, calendars, institutional

CONTINUED

history, and idiosyncrasies of personality that make up the legislative system. Unwilling to risk failure, I set out to do just that and discovered I had a talent for it.

In short, I learned not only how to make a difference, but when, if, and to what degree a difference could be made. I have always held to the general if bedrock beliefs that the proper role of government is to provide the greatest good for the greatest number, while protecting minorities, especially unpopular and powerless ones, from the tyranny of the majority. What I have learned, however, is that in practice those beliefs translate into a wide range of actions, many of them far from ideal. For example, in the 1960s I successfully authored measures to provide state impact aid to poor, inner-city, and rural schools and to establish a statewide Child Health and Disability Prevention Program, which subsequently became the model for federal law and laws in other states. In the 1980s, however, the best I could do was to help hold funding cuts in such programs to a minimum. Both efforts made a difference to millions of California children, although the former was more personally rewarding than the latter.

That's what Bismarck meant when he described politics as "the art of the possible." The art of the good politician, on the other hand, is to discern what is possible and then accomplish it. It is a challenge unending but never boring, painful but also rewarding, tedious but simultaneously exhilarating. Meeting that challenge offers the most consistent opportunities to make a difference.

Willie Brown, a state representative in California for 35 years and longtime Speaker of the California Assembly, is now Mayor of San Francisco.

Start Now

2

A few people who are very wealthy or widely known for their athletic abilities or have achieved television stardom can enter politics at mid-life and succeed. But they are the exceptions. Michael Huffington spent $28 million of his own money in seeking a Senate seat in California—and lost. Peter Fitzgerald dipped into his family fortune and spent $15 million and became a United States Senator from Illinois. But even with their wealth both did not start as statewide candidates. Senator Fitzgerald served in the state senate in Illinois before he advanced, and Michael Huffington served in the U.S. House.

Ronald Reagan used his stardom to make political speeches for several years before he launched his career by becoming Governor of California.

But almost all of you who read these pages will not be blessed with great wealth or movie and television stardom. That won't stop you from succeeding—if you are willing to work at it. Both Paul Simon and Michael Dukakis started in the state legislature and gradually worked our way up the political ladder.

Whether you are 16 or 66 when you read this book, the time to start is now.

Ask yourself where you would like to live. That spot is likely to be your political base. Read about the history of that community and, if you can afford it, get a newspaper that covers the news of that area. Become aware of the little details there, like some of your friends are familiar with batting averages of baseball players. However, what you are preparing yourself for is not a chance to cheer for the Boston Red Sox or St. Louis Cardinals, but to participate in the exciting, real-life game of improving the lot of others.

If you are genuinely interested in entering political life, don't postpone doing the little things that will start to build your base for the future. At the very worst, if you do this now and later you decide to run a restaurant or become a carpenter or rancher or teacher or electrical engineer, the work you have done to prepare yourself for a life in politics will help you in ways neither you nor we can know precisely.

You do not have to wait until you are older and want to run for the city council or state legislature. You can learn leadership skills now. Perhaps you should run for student body president, or class president, or secretary of the Latin Club, or leader of the youth group where you attend religious services. Practicing democracy and learning the skills of leadership do not suddenly blossom when you achieve voting age. The other day Paul Simon met a fourth-grade class president. She was learning leadership skills at that age, even though she might not know what we are talking about when we use the phrase "leadership skills."

In starting now while you are young, you can utilize your time effectively. Most people don't do that. For example, the average American watches almost 20 hours of television a week. Leaders in any field (with the exception of the television industry) don't do that. Leaders—and that's what you will be in politics—learn that the most precious gift you have outside of good health is time. Use it wisely. Leaders are participants, not "couch potatoes."

You should also ask yourself why you want to get into politics. What really is your goal in life? If your aim is to make money, then choose a different field. Successful political life involves long hours but not great financial rewards. A few people who enter politics eager for quick money end up in prison. Protect your good name if money is your goal, and go into business or some other professional field.

Early in his political career, Paul spoke to a small graduating high school class of 26 in a rural community. At the beginning of the ceremony, he gave each of the graduates a small piece of paper and a pencil and asked them to write in a few words about what they wanted out

of life. About half wrote that they had not really thought about that. Of the remaining answers, the one word that came through most frequently: *happiness.* Let's substitute the word satisfaction for happiness because satisfaction is a more enduring quality. The reality is that you do not get satisfaction (more than temporarily) from amassing great wealth. Both of us know some mighty unhappy millionaires. You do not get satisfaction by gaining fame, though there are moments of satisfaction that come with that. It is nice to get that high school diploma, and perhaps a bachelor's degree from college, or even a doctorate in some field, but by themselves adding these things gives no more than temporary pleasure.

Satisfaction in life is not achieved by adding things, but by subtracting. What gives you satisfaction is when you take from yourself and give to others.

We mention this because, when we ask you to start thinking and planning and studying now, it is also important for you to answer the question of why you want to get into politics. Is it fun? Yes. Is it exciting? Yes. Is it hard work? Yes. Will the hard work be worth it for you? That depends on your motivation, your reason for getting into politics.

We don't want to paint a picture for you of political life that is so completely geared to helping others that only saints need apply. The two of us enjoyed being in public office and seeking it. We made mistakes. Sometimes that resulted in editorial criticism or harsh words from our political opponents. Sometimes the most bitter criticism resulted from the best things that we did. Politics is a "rough and tumble" game. But the tough moments and days are much easier to bear if you know your motivation for being in public office.

If your basic motivation is good, then we want and need you in politics, and you should start preparing yourself now.

However, you have to make a living after you leave school. What field should you enter? Ask yourself what you would like to do 10 years from now, outside of politics. That is important for two reasons.

First, while you may be the best-qualified candidate for public office since George Washington, you may lose. More than half the candidates do lose. You want to have an occupation you can fall back on to support yourself, and for many of you, also support a young family.

The second reason it is important is that there is a greater possibility that you will be outstanding in work you like than in work you do not enjoy. More people who are attorneys enter political life than from any other field. One of this book's authors, Michael Dukakis, represents that field. But if you are an unhappy lawyer, you are not likely to impress either your fellow attorneys or anyone else. Go into teaching or farming or maintaining a home or whatever arena most appeals to you. But start asking yourself questions about how you can use that field as a stepping stone into political life. We have known funeral directors and farmers in public office, as well as physicians and pharmacists, teachers and preachers, social workers and stockbrokers. Choose a field you like, preferably one where you have as much contact with the public as possible. And then plan, plan, plan.

Another way to prepare yourself is to read a biography of a political leader you admire. If it is a good biography, you will discover that man or woman has blemishes, just as we all do. You will also learn that the person who succeeds does not do so because he or she did not encounter obstacles. The person who succeeds does not let the obstacles stop the political effort. If you own the book you are reading, underline sentences or paragraphs that are meaningful to you, and then in six months or a year you can go back and review that book and be reminded of some important lessons.

Abraham Lincoln had just turned 23 when he announced for State Representative in the *Sangamo Journal*. Lincoln always had a touch of sadness in what he said, even when he achieved victories. Read Lincoln's carefully chosen words, not the words of a buoyant spirit:

Every man is said to have his peculiar ambition. Whether it be true or not, I can say for one that I have no other so great as that of being truly esteemed by my fellow men, by rendering myself worthy of their

esteem. How far I shall succeed in gratifying this ambition, is yet to be developed. I am young and unknown to many of you. I was born and have ever remained in the most humble walks of life. I have no wealthy or popular relations to recommend me. My case is thrown exclusively upon the independent voters of this county, and if elected they will have conferred a favor upon me, for which I shall be unremitting in my labors to compensate. But if the good people in their wisdom shall see fit to keep me in the background, I have been too familiar with disappointments to be very much chagrined.

—A. Lincoln, March 15, 1832.

Lincoln lost the election, but two years later he came back and won. It took courage for a 23-year-old from the tiny village of New Salem, Illinois, to run for the legislature in 1832. He received 277 votes of the 300 cast in New Salem—more votes than were cast that year in a small village in the northern part of Illinois called Chicago. But Lincoln did not do well in his district where he was not known. If he had started earlier and visited Springfield and the other places in his district to get acquainted, he probably would have won. You can profit by his mistake, and start now.

By starting now, you also gradually build yourself up emotionally for the day when you "take the plunge" and run for office. That takes courage, that big first official step. You can't sit around and wait for "the right time." Some people spend their whole lives waiting for the right time. At some point you have to do it, despite the advice of some of your friends, and you should be preparing for that time right now.

Starting in Elementary School

FEDERICO PEÑA

It seems that starting in elementary school, I believe it was in the fifth grade, my classmates started electing me class president. It occurred year after year, well into high school. I do not recall campaigning as such; it was more an annual ritual, as my fellow students probably felt comfortable in the belief that I would not do anything that would embarrass them. I did not realize it at the time, but looking back on those early "political" years, my parents and their parents obviously had an influence on my willingness "to serve."

How did I develop an interest in politics? My grandfather, Eduardo Peña, was a city councilman for 25 years in Laredo, Texas. We lived 200 miles to the south in Brownsville, but I clearly remember traveling to Laredo to visit my grandparents, and we always talked about grandfather walking from his home to City Hall to conduct the city's business. I thought he was doing this for his health, but I bet he was shaking hands and campaigning every step of his trip downtown.

As I grew older, my parents, Gustavo and Lucila, told us of the civic and political activities of our ancestors. My mother's family (Farias family) had an interesting and erudite involvement in political and civic affairs in south Texas. In fact, the founder of Laredo, Texas, Colonel Tomas Sanchez, was one of my ancestors. Another ancestor, Santos Benavides, was Mayor of Laredo in 1857 and served in the territorial legislature, which required him to ride his horse to the state capital. Thus my parents conveyed to all six of their children a sense that we should be involved in our community, that we should be proud of the long line of civic leaders in our family, and that public

service was something worthwhile. It must have been that early parental influence and the family history lessons of south Texas that subconsciously inspired me to become involved in student politics. (Of course, I would like to have believed that it was my obvious traits of leadership and charisma that rallied my classmates to my class presidencies . . . but I doubt it.)

My father was also concerned about civic and political affairs. I have a recollection of our family traveling north to the big city of Harlingen, Texas, to stand on a sidewalk to watch President Dwight Eisenhower drive past in a parade. I think I saw the top of his head for a split second, but it was a big day for our family indeed! There was an important message imparted to all the Peña children from that "presidential exposure." My father also became involved in local politics. I recall his support and work for one of the first Hispanic Mayors of Brownsville (Mayor Tony Gonzalez) and our weekly "cafecitos" with several civic leaders in the back room of Mayor Gonzalez's pharmacy. During these "coffees," I would listen to them discuss the issues of the day affecting the political life of Brownsville. Then Dad was appointed to the first Public Utility Board in Brownsville's history. The city fathers believed that the city should own its own utility system, and I remember my father staying up late after a hard day of work reading about German power generation plants and trying to decide which were the best to be purchased for the city.

Parents and family do have an influence on their children's interests and involvement in community affairs. Clearly mine were role models. Their actions and kitchen table discussions about politics obviously encouraged me to serve my community in later years.

But where elementary school elections were one thing, getting involved in a real campaign was another. And so the opportunity arose one year when I

CONTINUED

returned home from college to discover that a wonderful woman named Frances "Sissy" Farenthold had decided to run for Governor of Texas against the second Dolph Briscoe. For a woman to run for governor in Texas was to make "real" history, but it helped pave the way for someone such as Ann Richards to win years later. At any rate, Mr. Briscoe beat "Sissy" in the primary election in my home county, Cameron County. Somehow my brothers and I took up her cause, opened a campaign headquarters, organized college students in the county, and produced an upset victory with "Sissy" winning in Cameron County in the general election. Unfortunately, she lost statewide. But we reveled in the knowledge that we had beaten the local "establishment," we refused to provide gasoline and tires to the "politiceras" (those wonderful Hispanic women who could guarantee you a certain number of votes for a few automotive improvements), and we organized a new breed of younger and more passionate voters in south Texas. While we lost the larger statewide gubernatorial election, we won some self-confidence and developed a belief that politics could make a positive difference in our lives.

In addition to my family's interest in civic affairs, I also was influenced by President John F. Kennedy. He was elected while I was in high school. He inspired me to look to public service as a noble endeavor, where one could rally our nation to send an American to the moon, to fight discrimination, or to help those in need. But when I later attended the University of Texas in 1964, a group of friends and I became disillusioned with campus politics (it seemed that fraternities and sororities controlled campus politics), and so we ran "Mickey Mouse" for student body president. I would walk around campus dressed in a blue blazer, white gloves and slacks, and a paper-mâché head of "Mickey," accompanied by a ragtime band. We had a ridiculous platform (free cheese in the student union, etc.), but we were

making a serious point about the superficiality of university politics. We struck a responsive cord, and many students took the message to heart. "Mickey" placed a respectable third place in the final election. I believe our satirical campaign changed campus politics because future candidates started to address issues more relevant to the broader campus community and not simply the interests of a few organized groups.

After graduating from law school, I eventually made my way to Denver, Colorado, as a civil rights lawyer. I helped draft and lobby bilingual legislation for the state legislature. When Representative Ruben Valdez ran for statewide office, a few legislators encouraged me to run for his legislative seat in North Denver. I ran a grassroots campaign and was elected to two terms in the Colorado House of Representatives and served as Minority Leader of that body at the age of 33. Later I was elected Mayor of Denver, served eight years, and then asked by President Clinton to serve as Secretary of Transportation (1993–97) and Secretary of Energy (1998–99). The rest, as they say, is "history."

When students ask me how they can become involved in politics, I explain that I was blessed to have parents and grandparents who encouraged me. I was inspired by the young and dynamic President John F. Kennedy. My advice to anyone interested in politics is to become involved in a local campaign, whether a city council race or school board election or even a referendum about which one cares deeply. Take an interest in school politics, volunteer to work for a congressional candidate, or run for office yourself. You should have a compelling reason to do so, for example, to change the policies of your school, to make your neighborhood safer, and yes, to elect a new President. I emphasize that a few people can make an enormous difference and can galvanize public opinion. My work with a handful of people in Sissy Farenthold's campaign or the small number of us who challenged campus

CONTINUED

politics at my university are cases in which a few people made a difference. Once involved, your experience and commitment will grow. There will be victories and losses, but always the satisfaction that you made the effort to make your community better. Who knows, these experiences may someday take you from a small town like Brownsville to the breathtaking steps of our nation's capital.

Federico Peña, formerly Mayor of Denver, was Secretary of Transportation and Secretary of Energy during the Clinton administration.

Personal Political Narratives

"How Did You Get into Politics?"

AL SIMPSON

One heckuva good question! And a good answer is—my dear dad had politics coursing through his veins, and dinner table conversations were often filled with dazzling tales of intrigue, partisanship, excitement, treachery, success, kindness and harshness—all the things that go to make up life itself!

Dad ran for the United States Senate in 1940, when I was nine years old. He lost big. I was heartbroken—so was he. He took off the summer months of 1941 in order to close up his deceased father's law practice in Jackson, Wyoming, and those were great times in the life of my dear parents and brother, Peter, and me. Pop's loss was our gain! He knew it, too. So he waited until 1954, when he decided to run for Governor of Wyoming. By then, brother Pete and I were 23 and 22 years of age. We both worked hard for him, and he won—by a whisker! He served with guts, courage, and strength. He ran for reelection in 1958, and he lost—a principal reason being because he was not in favor of capital punishment. Try that one out in the vigilante country days of old Wyoming!

But it showed his authentic, core values and thus, when he ran for the U.S. Senate in 1962—at the age of 65—he won by the largest margin ever given to a U.S. Senate candidate up to that time. Quite a history. You have to have someone like that in your life—that was my Dad.

So when it came time for me, at age 33, I ran for the Wyoming legislature in 1964 and was elected and served 13 years. I loved it. I loved legislating. Some people are cut out to be administrators, Governors, Mayors, executives, President, not me! I couldn't administer my way out of a paper bag!

CONTINUED

But I loved legislating. I loved the hearings. I loved the amending process. I loved the reading. I loved personally crafting legislation (for in the Wyoming legislature, I had no legislative aide). I loved the floor work and the conference committees, the whole works! One accomplishment that I am most proud of is my work on immigration reform. It had not been touched for 30 years. Ron Mazzoli, a great pal and a Democrat from the Third District of Kentucky, and I first put together the Simpson–Mazzoli bill, also later known as the Simpson–Rodino bill, in order to get a handle on illegal immigration and try to get sensible again with regard to both legal and illegal immigration.

I also worked hard on the Clean Air Act, Superfund legislation, high-level nuclear waste, and many judicial nominations. In all of those, I hope I "made a difference."

The most memorable character I ever met in political life was my father. He was my inspiration. He had it all: smart, wise, witty, warm, and when someone tried to distort the type of man he was, he became, perhaps best described as—"prickly!" Sometimes, he had a hell of a good temper, too— passed on to his progeny and that has been a tough one for me to keep in check from time to time!

He and my wonderful mother both influenced me because I saw them serve as Governor and First Lady of Wyoming and then U.S. Senator and "wife of," and they did it with such class. It never changed them. Who they were when they left Cody, Wyoming, was who they were when they came back. And that's quite remarkable in Washington—for those who travel the high road of humility in Washington, D.C., are not troubled by heavy traffic! I have always said, "If you didn't know who you are before you go to Washington, it's sure a poor place to try to find out!"

What does it mean to "hold public office"? Just that. You "hold it"—in trust for the people who sent you there. Nothing more and nothing less. The main responsibilities of someone in public office? Use your head. Do your home-work. Don't read the polls. Just figure they sent you there because they themselves were busy raising their families and working every day, doing their business and living their lives—and they sent you off to do the work and expected you to use your brain and your common sense. I am not the first public servant sent off to do that, in these paraphrased words of Edmund Burke.

If you are a legislator, your principal job is to pass laws that are understand-able to the governed. That's what I always tried to do.

What does it mean to be a citizen? It too means just that. It means that you are not a member of the AARP first or the NRA first, or the AFL-CIO first—you're a citizen of the United States first. And if you've forgotten that, then we're all in for a lot of trouble!

The responsibilities of a citizen? Pay attention. Learn to take part or get taken apart. Democracy is not a spectator sport. Get in the game! It doesn't take any brains to be a continual critic or sit around and whine. If you don't like what's going on in your government, "Get in and get wet all over!" Whether it's the city council, school board, county commission, state legislature—you name it.

What hopes for the future in the next decade? Plenty of 'em! I think young people will begin to pay more attention. I am very pleased with a group called Third Millennium in New York. They charge nine bucks dues, one buck more than the AARP. Any young person between 18 and 35 should get in the fray. Here's a place to start. They are concerned with the next generational

CONTINUED

cycle rather than the next election cycle. They must do this in order to avoid the intergenerational sex scrapping that will surely come in the years ahead. As for the students I meet as I travel around the country, whether at Northeastern or Southern Illinois University or Harvard or the University of Wyoming or Berkeley: they are impressive. The country is in good hands with the young people I have met since I left the U.S. Senate—and even before.

The issues that loom the largest in the years ahead are the ones that generate the most anguish—and embody all of the elements of emotion, fear, guilt, and racism. The central issues: the population of the Earth. Here's the hard one. It matters not how much propellant there is in the bottom of a shaving cream can or whether methane gas from cows will destroy the Earth; the issue is simply that human beings will destroy the Earth—for they have that rapacious capacity. They have done it in certain societies now gone. The population of the Earth has doubled since 1940 and before that, from the beginning of man until now—doubled—and it will double again by the year 2056. Can't miss. There's where we must ponder how many footprints will fit on the face of the Earth?

Final tip! Beware of the extremists on both sides of every issue, whether gun control, abortion, ethnicity, religion, or nuclear energy.

Stay away from the "Hell no, we won't glow" crew and the "Nobody's ever been killed" bunch—they're both off the rail. Then as to abortion—a most serious issue—it hopefully can be resolved by just one sentence, at least in my political party. We should be able to say, "Abortion is a deeply intimate and personal decision and out of respect for each other it will not be part of our party platform."

There's so much to do here in this country and so many of us here to do it. "To do a thing, be at it!" And always remember again, it doesn't take any brains to be an eternal critic—such a critic is a product of creativity not his own. And don't forget the first definition of politics, so that you don't get swept away in a rosy glow of idealism.

Here it is, "In politics, there are no right answers—only a continuing flow of compromises among groups; resulting in a changing, cloudy, and ambiguous series of public decisions—where appetite and ambition compete openly with knowledge and wisdom."

That's it.

And if you're plumb fed up with politics and partisanship and you keep on moaning and whining, I earnestly suggest that you move to a country where they don't have any politics or partisanship—then write me a note in about six months and tell me how much fun you're having. You won't like it. You would have lost your freedom, your precious right of expression, and so many rights that you now take for granted in this great country.

And remember this: "If you're damned if you do and damned if you don't—then do! The world is waiting for you to do! I'll be watching, too!"

Al Simpson served in the Wyoming legislature for 13 years as a Republican. In 1978, he was elected to the United States Senate, where he became one of the leading figures in the Republican Party. He retired in 1997.

3 | **Pick a Party**

M any Americans are uncomfortable with the notion that two major political parties dominate the U.S. national scene.

They take pride in their independence. "I vote the candidate," they say, "not the party. I'm an Independent." There is nothing inherently wrong with that kind of attitude. In fact, we have two Independent governors serving in office at this moment: Angus King of Maine and Jesse Ventura of Minnesota, both living proof that you don't have to be a Republican or a Democrat to succeed in American politics. Mike Dukakis remembers one political campaign in heavily Democratic Massachusetts when the Republican candidate for Governor, John Volpe, used the slogan, "Vote the Man; Vote Volpe." It worked, too. Volpe was elected and reelected and subsequently went on to become Secretary of Transportation in the Nixon administration and U.S. Ambassador to Italy.

On the other hand, political parties are a fact of life in American politics, and your chances of doing something significant in politics are usually going to be much better if you become active in the party of your choice.

That does not mean that third-party movements in this country have not been important. "Fighting Bob" LaFollette of Wisconsin and the Progressive movement had a profound effect on politics and public policy during the early years of the twentieth century. Ross Perot's focus on deficit reduction in the 1992 presidential campaign forced Bill Clinton and George Bush to address the issue seriously, and Perot deserves at least some of the credit for the fact that we are enjoying unprecedented surpluses for the first time in decades.

What normally happens in this country, however, is that if a third party has some interesting ideas that begin to have an impact, the major parties quickly absorb and incorporate them into their own platforms. That is one of the reasons third parties have a relatively short life in American political history.

The two major political parties play an essential role in American politics. They bring like-minded people together. They give organizational strength to the system. They adopt platforms and help to educate voters on the issues. They provide a political home for those who seek to become active in politics. They run caucuses and conventions that are essential parts of the system. They get people registered and help to get out the vote. Without them, the American political system would be weakened.

That doesn't mean that everything they do is wonderful. After all, it is a rare American, even a party loyalist, who agrees with everything his or her party favors or, more particularly, the way our parties are run. Both of us were rebels within our party in our youth because we believed in more open and accountable party leadership.

M any argue that there isn't "a dime's worth of difference" between our two major political parties. Because legislators in our system are elected independently, we do not have the sharp divisions you find in most parliamentary systems. However, party members of the U.S. House and Senate are more likely to vote with their party than 40 or 50 years ago, though it is still true that a moderate Republican, such as Senator Olympia Snowe of Maine, will vote more like Senator Charles Robb of Virginia, a moderate Democrat, than like Senator Phil Gramm of Texas, a more conservative Republican. But a few decades ago liberals such as Wayne Morse of Oregon or John Lindsay of New York called themselves Republican, as did the most conservative members, and Democrats included liberal Senator Hubert Humphrey of Minnesota and conservative Senator Richard Russell of Georgia.

Today the parties are more cohesive ideologically than a generation ago. Most would agree that a fundamental difference between the parties is that Democrats are generally more willing to use government to achieve social and economic goals than Republicans. The Republican Party, by contrast, emphasizes the importance of private sector and voluntary solutions to many of the challenges facing the nation.

However, these general descriptions are not always accurate. Republicans, for example, are more willing to use big government on defense and national security issues. Democrats generally favor less government intervention in what they believe are essentially private and personal issues such as abortion and sex between consenting adults.

Nevertheless, on most major issues Democrats tend to be more "interventionist" than Republicans, and whether one party prevails politically often depends on whether the American people believe that it is essential for the government to get actively involved in a major public issue. The debate over a "Patient's Bill of Rights" is a case in point. Both parties have proposed legislation on the subject, but the Democrats want tougher regulation and more government intervention than most of the Republicans. Democrats are more likely to favor a national healthcare system that should be required by the federal government than are Republicans.

The reality is that a balance is needed on most matters. Having a strong voice from both political parties sometimes weakens legislation, but it often refines it so that the public interest is better served than if either political party had too much dominance.

You don't have to make a decision now about what party you will join if you want to get actively involved in politics. But you should be getting to know local party leaders and legislators; attending party meetings; and beginning to decide which party's philosophy best seems to fit your philosophy and your values.

When you do plunge into partisan activities, you'll find that, with rare exceptions, the local party organization will welcome you. Those local committees are part of a network that starts at the top with the Republican and Democratic National Committees; a state central committee in each state elected by Republican or Democratic voters in

primaries or caucuses; and local or county party committees who are composed of party activists elected in those same primaries or caucuses.

Again, with rare exceptions you will find your local political organization eager to enlist your energy and your enthusiasm. If it is not, you may want to run against it. Mike Dukakis won his first political office of any importance as a third-year law student when, unhappy with what he perceived to be a rather sleepy and inactive party organization in his hometown, he organized a slate of 35 reform-minded Democrats. They ran against the incumbent organization and won, and he became the local party chair.

What do local party organizations do? If they are any good, they recruit party volunteers; assign them to election districts and precincts; urge them to walk the streets and get to know their neighbors; encourage them to educate their precinct's voters on the issues and why their party has the right answers; register those who are not registered to vote; organize phone banks; and get out the vote on election day.

There are Young Republican and Young Democratic organizations in every state and college Democratic and college Republican organizations on the nation's campuses. There is ample opportunity to get deeply and actively involved in the party of your choice and develop the skills you need to be an effective party organizer and, ultimately, a fine public servant.

It is in grassroots organizing for our parties that most of us got our start. If you have talent for the job and a high level of energy and enthusiasm, you will be encouraged to take on more and more responsibility. That may lead to managing a campaign, and then perhaps at some point you will throw your hat in the ring and run for office yourself. Early experience as a party worker at the grassroots level is excellent preparation for a try at public office. You will understand more about the mechanics of campaigning. You will learn how to identify friendly voters, set up an effective precinct organization, schedule your time, appreciate what all those volunteers are sacrificing to

work for you because you were there once, and raise the funds, preferably at the grassroots, that you will need to win.

You will also learn that it is possible to run a good and winning campaign without selling your soul to big campaign contributors. Both of us had long careers in public life. Both of us had to raise large sums of money to do it. Both of us managed to raise that money primarily from thousands and thousands of small donors at the grassroots, not from big money political action committees.

How do you do that? By spending a lot of time in living rooms and at backyard barbecues where the tab may only be $25 or $50. But the people who come to these kinds of events and contribute that kind of money will work hard for you at the grassroots if they are convinced that you are the kind of person they want representing them. If with their help you are elected, you enter public office obligated not to special interests but to the thousands of good people who dug deeply into their pockets for a modest contribution because they had a chance to meet and get to know you in or near their homes, and they came to trust you.

However, both of us believe that the present system of campaign finance with its increasing reliance on hundreds of millions of dollars in so-called "soft" money is a disgrace and must be changed. Our unhappiness and frustration at Congress's failure to reform the system did not, however, stop us from running—and running successfully—for major political office. Don't let it discourage you either. You can run for political office in this country, raise the necessary funds in the right way, and win.

What worries both of us, and what we hope you will help to change, is the increasing failure of both major political parties to invest time and money in genuine grassroots organizing and campaigning. Both parties have been too quick to buy into the notion that politics these days is a matter of political consultants, big money, and expensive TV commercials and that old-fashioned grassroots organizing and campaigning doesn't make a difference.

Don't you believe it. There is good research that tells us that a first-rate, grassroots campaign can make a difference of 8 or 10 points in the outcome. There aren't too many political contests that are won by more than that, and we are living testimonials to that fact. A swing of just four points in 1988 would have made Mike Dukakis President of the United States.

Hard work in the local precincts can pay dividends on election day. It also is important to the future of American democracy. Those of us who have been in politics for a long time in this country are troubled by the declining voter turnout and increasing voter cynicism.

We are convinced that one of the reasons for this cynicism is that in too many American communities politics no longer has a human face. Nobody rings a doorbell. Nobody calls you. There is little evidence of local party activity. Even local television news is paying less and less attention to candidates and campaigns.

Instead, we are being fed a steady diet of 30-second attack commercials cooked up by high-priced consultants whose pay often depends on how many commercials they run on television. No wonder more and more American voters are cynical. No wonder they seem less inclined to go to the polls to vote.

That can change if party activists walk the streets, ring doorbells, get to know their neighbors, put up house signs, and get people to the polls with a coherent message about what their party and their candidates intend to do about the important issues facing the nation.

You can be an important part of this grassroots democracy, and once you get used to making the rounds, you will thoroughly enjoy it. Between us we've rung thousands of doorbells. We learned much climbing up and down those stairs, and we had fun doing it. There's nothing like getting someone out of the bathtub, as Mike once did, to send you on your way chuckling. And she voted for Mike, too!

The Heart of Political Change

DIANNE FEINSTEIN

I've held a number of positions during the course of my own public life: California Women's Board of Terms and Parole, president of the San Francisco Board of Supervisors, Mayor of San Francisco and finally, U.S. Senator. Each has had its own challenges. But throughout my life, my principal dedication has been to do the best I can to see that government works for the people.

One of the defining moments in my life came on November 27, 1978. I was president of the Board of Supervisors, but had lost two bids to become Mayor. My husband, Bert, had died of cancer the previous April. That morning, I arrived at City Hall and informed some of the reporters that I had decided not to run for Mayor again and would leave politics at the end of my term.

A short time later, I heard shots down the hall, ran to Supervisor Harvey Milk's office, and found him on the floor. I reached for a pulse, but felt only a bullet hole. It was clear he was dead. I subsequently learned Mayor George Moscone had also been shot and killed. The killer was former Supervisor Dan White, whose subsequent conviction on the lesser charge of manslaughter led to the "White Night" riot in May 1979.

I thus became Mayor as a result of assassination. I held that post through the end of Mayor Moscone's term and was reelected twice. It was a very trying time in San Francisco. Only nine days earlier, more than 900 men, women, and children, most of them San Franciscans, had drunk cyanide-laced Kool-Aid and died in Jonestown, Guyana.

It was as if the world had gone mad. As the new Mayor, I was determined that I needed to do the things to reassure the city, provide some consistency, put the bricks back together again.

From that nonpartisan experience, I drew my greatest political lesson. That lesson is that the heart of political change, believe it or not, is at the center of the political spectrum. That the more diverse we become as a society, the more government is run from the center, and the more government must do not what is "politically correct," but what works and solves the problem at hand.

And if you work from the center of the political spectrum, you can listen to the right, you can listen to the left, you can make judgments as to what is the best thing for all people. And I did that as mayor for nine solid years.

I am reminded of my uncle, who used to take me down to City Hall on Monday afternoons to what he called the "Board of Stupidvisors." He would say to me, "Dianne, you get an education, and you do the job right." And for some reason, it stuck.

For those of us who hold elected office, governing in this complex and diverse country can often be very difficult. If we've learned anything from the past, it's that it takes all of us who treasure our nation's beauty and the character of our people to be mindful and respectful of one another.

Every day we are called upon to put aside our animosities to search together for common ground, not how we are different, but how we are similar. We must learn to settle differences, before they fester and become real problems.

Our culture in the United States is one that values tolerance and forbearance with an enduring spirit of democracy. The right of an individual to speak out, the right of an individual in combination with due process of law to live and

CONTINUED

grow and thrive in a society. Ensuring these rights—that's my purpose, and every day I must rededicate myself to that ideal. I fall short a lot of the days, but nonetheless the dedication and the rededication must take place.

Coming from a nonpartisan political office, I've found the intense, mean-spirited partisanship that I've encountered as a U.S. Senator deeply disturbing. I've seen five years of steady investigation and a determination "to get" the President of the United States and a meanness of spirit that I never thought would be present in our nation's capital.

Unfortunately, I sincerely believe that the continuation of this mean-spiritedness has the potential to destroy the two-party process in the sense that more people will register "decline to state" and say "a pox on both your houses."

Yes, I am a Democrat, and I know what I value as a Democrat. But it is imperative that I be able to work out real solutions to real problems with Democrats and Republicans alike. I bring my ethics; I bring my basic philosophy; I bring my morality; I bring whatever I've learned; and, yes, I bring my party to the equation. But my job is to work across the aisle. That's the path I've chosen, and it's the way I believe I can be most constructive in serving the people I represent.

Dianne Feinstein, formerly Mayor of San Francisco, was the first woman elected to the United States Senate from California. She has served in the Senate since 1992.

Personal Political Narratives

A Party That Represented My Beliefs

KAY BAILEY HUTCHISON

My path to the U.S. Senate is one I could not have charted as a young woman, but each unexpected detour has enriched the journey. What I've learned along the way is that it's less important to know what to do for a living than what you want to accomplish with your life. Principle, not expedience, should be the star that guides you.

My journey began after three years of law school at the University of Texas. As a young adult, I was in a hurry, eager to begin a career in law. I'd skipped my senior year of college to get to law school sooner. Law degree in hand, I hit life's first brick wall: major Houston law firms did not hire women in 1969. After three months of interviews, I struck out.

One day, after yet another disappointing interview experience, I was driving home past the local NBC affiliate, KPRC-TV, in Houston. On a lark, I stopped, went in, and asked the receptionist if I could speak to someone about being a news reporter.

"You mean you'd like to talk to the news director," she said.

"Sure." I knew nothing about the business of journalism, but that sounded right.

The news director, Mr. Ray Miller, was intrigued with the idea of a woman news reporter with a law degree. Not only were there no women reporters on Houston TV, but he said he'd never had a lawyer apply, either!

CONTINUED

Ray wanted to open the first local TV capitol bureau to cover the state legislature—since I was a lawyer, he handed me the assignment. The experiment worked, and other stations soon followed suit. Apparently, the woman news reporter experiment wasn't a bad idea, either, because the other Houston stations hired women reporters within a year.

In 1971, after two years as a journalist, my life took another unanticipated turn when I was asked to consider making a move from covering the legislature to joining it. The Republican Party chairman in Harris County—where Houston is located—urged me to run. Although my background was not political, my father had taught me to give back to the community. Elective office was true to that teaching. I'd observed the legislature for two years and felt confident I was up to the task (at the ripe old age of 28).

I first had to decide which party best represented my beliefs. As a news reporter, I did not vote in the party primaries in Austin because I wanted to maintain objectivity. I thought about the issues that mattered to me: limiting government involvement in our daily lives; the need to reduce the tax burden and create a climate in which business can thrive and employees prosper; and the importance of individuals taking personal responsibility. I felt these views were best represented by the principles of the Republican Party.

I also felt that a more balanced two-party system would be healthier for Texas. My father felt it was a civic duty to support both parties, and he used to send small checks to both the Democratic and Republican state parties. In 1971, though, the Texas state legislature was vastly Democratic, with just 10 Republicans in the 150-member House.

So I became a Republican and voted in my first Republican primary—for myself, to represent District 90. I was on my way to Austin!

I was the first Republican woman elected to the Texas House. There were five women and 13 Republicans for this 1973 session. I found that the women in the legislature, regardless of party, worked together to bring issues forward.

Also affecting my legislative priorities was the district I represented, which was in Texas's largest city. The legislature was in a transition from a mostly rural to a mixed urban-rural representation, and many of the concerns of my constituents needed to be addressed.

In two terms in the legislature, I'm proudest of the following accomplishments:

I brought mass transit to Texas. It was difficult to convince a rural-dominated legislature that cities needed taxing authority to improve public transportation. But the matter was vital for Houston and other cities. I worked hard over two sessions of the legislature to win the right for cities to add a one-cent sales tax to be used for mass transit. Today, some of our nation's best mass transit systems are in Texas.

The Bailey–Weddington bill to create fair treatment for rape victims. The women of the House (four Democrats and myself, the only Republican) united behind this long-overdue legislation. At the time, victims of rape were often treated as if they were the criminals. Our legislation put Texas in the vanguard of states for victims' rights by extending the statute of limitations during which a rape can be reported and prohibiting courtroom testimony about the victim in most cases.

The Bailey County Historical Commissions bill, to safeguard the state's history. Its particular impact has been the preservation of scores of historic county courthouses that serve as repositories of the unique heritage of early Texas settlers.

CONTINUED

After leaving the legislature and serving in Washington as the Vice Chairman of the National Transportation Safety Board for President Gerald Ford, I settled in Dallas with my husband Ray—whom I'd met as a fellow legislator in the state House—and became general counsel for Republic Bank Holding Company. I later ran for Congress (I lost), went into business for myself, buying and running a candy manufacturing company, and started a bank. I also became active in Dallas civic affairs and thought I was finished in politics, enjoying private entrepreneurship.

These years prepared me well for my eventual return to public service. I saw how government at every level impacts small businesses, the engine of prosperity in America. I've known many public officials who have little experience outside of politics and run for office before clarifying the principles on which to base their governing philosophy. (In 1971, I was in this category.) Our democracy is strengthened when officeholders have learned the lessons of everyday life in America before seeking to represent others.

In 1990, I reentered public life by winning election to the office of Texas State Treasurer. Spurred on by what I'd seen in the private sector, I had two priorities: opposing a proposed state income tax and limiting the amount of debt the state could issue. With great support in the state legislature, my debt limit proposal passed. Also, after a vigorous public campaign by both sides, we opponents prevailed, and the legislature passed a constitutional amendment prohibiting an income tax.

To my surprise, in 1993, the newly elected President Clinton named Texas Senator Lloyd Bentsen as his Treasury Secretary. After a lot of encouragement from supporters, I decided to throw my hat in the ring for the open primary for the special election to replace him. More than 20 candidates from both parties were on the ballot, including two Republican Congressmen

CONTINUED

and the incumbent Democratic Senator who'd been appointed as Secretary Bentsen's interim replacement. To my greater surprise, I won.

As a Senator, my goals remain much the same as when I entered public life in 1973. I want to preserve the American economic miracle by creating favorable conditions for jobs and prosperity. That means easing the tax burden, cutting wasteful spending, and keeping the budget balanced. I'm very committed to a strong national defense. We must also confront one of our most vexing problems: saving Social Security for those who depend upon it today and will be paying into it over the next few decades.

Young women today have more opportunities than I ever thought possible when I was growing up in a small Texas town. America is the greatest country in the world for women to achieve their dreams and for men and women alike to seize the opportunities freedom provides. And our best days are yet to come.

Kay Bailey Hutchison, a Republican and native of Dallas, was the first woman elected to the U.S. Senate from Texas.

4 | **Become a Student!**

" **I** 'm already a student," we can hear you say. We're suggesting something different, something practical.

In an election year, there will be political rallies and every year meetings of governmental units where you would be welcomed—not many young people usually attend—and where you can come to know the process better and at the same time evaluate candidates and officials close-up. You can determine whether you would enjoy being part of the process.

Reading your local newspaper is a good way to keep up on the issues internationally, nationally, and in your community. As you follow the local scene, you will read about city council meetings, sessions of the local school board, and deliberations of your county board. Depending on where you live, you may find park district board meetings or meetings of other governmental units. Illinois even has Mosquito Abatement Districts!

In the county seat city where you live, there will be trials, probably in the courthouse, called that because that is where the local courts ordinarily meet. Find out from the sheriff's office or the prosecuting attorney's office when trials are being held and what is coming up that might be of interest to you. Most of the focus of this book is on the legislative and executive functions of government and how we become participants there, but our courts are a third important branch of our democratic system. Attending even part of one trial will give you a little better understanding of how our judicial system works.

What can you learn by attending a political rally? A city council meeting? A trial? Won't these things be boring?

Once you start becoming familiar with the players and the issues, any of these events can sometimes provide first-class entertainment. As a young reporter, Paul Simon attended a city council meeting of a small town when, in the midst of a controversy, the Mayor shouted at his council, "You're all a bunch of thieves." The heated debate that followed this unstaged event makes the staged events of the World Wrestling Federation look tame and dull. Mike Dukakis often said that he would have paid an admission fee to listen to some of the debates in the representative town meeting, in which he served in his hometown.

T he primary reason for attending these proceedings is not entertainment but to learn more how your government functions and whether you would like to play an active role in it. (You might also ask your teacher or instructor if you can receive extra credit for attending some of these events.)

If you're a little shy, ask a friend or two to go with you to one political rally or one of the meetings. After you have forced yourself to do it once, you will find it easier the next time. That's true of much political activity. The first time you go door-to-door either as a candidate or supporting a candidate, knocking on that first door or ringing a doorbell—it is amazing how many doorbells don't work—will be difficult, and then it will quickly become much easier for you. The first time you stand before your class or at a meeting to ask a question, or make some comments, you will be nervous. The second time you will be a little less nervous, and gradually you will probably feel at ease before most audiences.

As you attend political rallies and meetings of governmental bodies, ask yourself a few questions: Is the noisiest person the wisest? Who really is listened to by others because he or she offers substance? Which candidate or officeholder does his or her homework?

And listen. Listen to what speakers say at a political event but also listen to what people say in response to those who present themselves. At a city council meeting listen to what the members say, listen to the reports from the police chief and the city attorney and the water manager, but also listen to the comments of the few—and it is usually a few—citizens who are there as observers. Why are the observers there? Do they want to sell the city something, or seek a favor from the city council? How many of those who do not belong to the city council or work for the city are there simply to see how their government operates, to find out whether it is serving them well?

As you look at the membership of the city council or school board or county board, does it reflect at least partially your area? How many women are serving? If your area is one-fourth African American or one-fourth Latino, are they here? Why are these things important? If it is a political rally you are attending, does the audience reflect the diversity that is in your community? If one of the candidates tells an off-color joke, or attempts to get a laugh from the audience by relating something that makes fun of another race or religion, or tells a story that ridicules gays or disabled people or Poles or any other group, the storyteller will usually get a laugh from an audience, and he or she is usually too insensitive to note that it does not please everyone, and with some in the audience there is a forced, uneasy laugh. A candidate who uses profanity in public speaking, or four-letter words that aim to shock or entertain an audience, may shock and entertain, but he or she rarely picks up supporters or votes. What are you learning about the importance of getting along with everyone, and understanding others, at these meetings and rallies?

You don't need to have traveled the globe or even to different parts of the United States to learn more about the rest of the world. You can find opportunities to broaden your understanding of different cultures and backgrounds right now in your school and community. Introduce yourself to people of different racial and ethnic backgrounds who you may have in class but have never spoken with before. Seek out students who are new to your school and make them feel welcome.

Since less than 2 percent of Americans are farmers, most of you who read these words are not farmers. How about getting a few of you together and contacting a local farm organization or a farmer you know and telling him or her that you would like a one- or two-hour

tour of a farm to understand better how farmers operate. "Traveling" to see people in your area costs much less than going to Europe or Asia or Africa and can be as rewarding and enriching for you.

Meet as many people as you can at a rally or government meeting. When you meet someone, ask his or her name, and then repeat it, "I'm happy to meet you, Jane Smith." It is a small attention that you pay people that creates a positive impression in their minds about you. There is an old saying, "You never have too many friends." That is true in politics; that is true also in life. Ask yourself why some people make a better impression on you than others do. What can you learn from those whose conduct and actions somehow please you more? If a public official impresses you favorably, after checking with your instructor, why not invite him or her to visit one of your classes and tell the students the function of the office and then answer questions.

All of this may sound a little overwhelming. You're not sure you're up to the task. It's not that bad, but it does take a little extra effort. The difference between those who become leaders and those who do not is that "little extra effort." Just do these things one step at a time, and you will find it is not that difficult. These are suggestions, and we think from our experiences good suggestions. But start down this path, and then you can make your own trail. An early American writer, James Russell Lowell, wrote: "He who waits to have his task marked out shall die and leave his errand unfulfilled." Your errand may be political leadership. At least look at that option carefully.

If you take a few of these steps outlined here, you will be "hooked for life" with an interest in government. Even if you never become a candidate or play a major role in political life, you are not likely to become part of the 51 percent of the potential voting population that did not even vote in the presidential election in 1996. Participation is good for you, and it's good for our nation.

But let us make another guess: After attending your first rally or official board meeting, you will come away somewhat impressed by the caliber of the men and women there. After attending several such events, you will make a startling discovery: While the men and women there have more background and experience than you do, largely because they have lived longer, they don't have more native ability than you do. Those who emerge in positions of leadership in this nation and other nations are often people of average ability who are willing to work a little harder, who for one reason or another have more of a sense of dedication. They make that "little extra effort."

The two of us have had the good fortune to know the leaders of this country and several other countries. The most impressive among them are not necessarily those who are brilliant. The most impressive are those who have somewhat above-average ability, but they use that ability with courage, with hard work, and with a willingness to reach out to help others. You can be among the future leaders. Enroll in the unusual "study course" we outline in this chapter, and your chances of emerging as a leader are excellent.

Personal Political Narratives

From Activist to Elected Office

WILMA MANKILLER

Politics has always been a part of my life. When I was growing up, my parents and siblings rarely argued about mundane household issues. They argued endlessly about politics and issues affecting our community.

While my early childhood was spent in a remote, very rural Oklahoma Cherokee community, we moved to California when I was 10 years of age. From adolescence to adulthood, my family and I lived at Hunter's Point, a rough housing project in San Francisco. In California my father became a longshoreman, a union advocate, and a shop steward. He also became involved with the local Native American community center, where political discussions were the norm. Also, just living in an isolated, predominately African-American community was a political experience. Young people from East Oakland and Hunter's Point began the groundwork for what ultimately became the Black Panther Party by providing free breakfasts for children in the community.

During the late 1960s and early 1970s, the San Francisco Bay Area was a mecca for civil rights, the women's movement, and massive anti-war demonstrations. A controversial alternative community was created in San Francisco's Haight-Ashbury district by mostly young, white, middle-class people. The air was electric with change. Even the music was changing as Janis Joplin and Jimi Hendrix brought their wildly creative sound to the West Coast. Anything seemed possible.

In 1969, a dozen Native American students occupied Alcatraz Island in the San Francisco Bay, citing a treaty that provided for the return of unused

CONTINUED

federal land to tribal people. Four of my siblings—two brothers and two sisters—joined the occupation, and I became involved as well. Charismatic Native American leaders spoke about things I felt but could not articulate or name. They talked about treaty rights and how we could rebuild whole, healthy communities again by looking to our own culture for solutions to contemporary problems. Alcatraz was a watershed political experience for me. From the time I stepped off the boat at Alcatraz almost 30 years ago, I have been actively engaged in the world around me, sometimes as a volunteer or a human rights advocate and for 10 years as an elected tribal leader.

Though my interest and participation in politics evolved over many decades, my transformation from activist to candidate for elective office was swift and unexpected. Our former principal chief, Ross Swimmer, asked me to become his running mate in the June, 1983, Cherokee election. Initially I declined. I could not imagine how I would make the transition from founding director of the Cherokee Nation community development department to a candidate for political office. The Cherokee Nation, with a population approaching 200,000, is the second largest tribal government in the United States. While most voting members reside within the boundaries of the Cherokee Nation, now Northeastern Oklahoma, thousands of Cherokee voters are scattered throughout the United States. Running for tribal office is much like running for Congress, or even a national post. It is a fairly mainstream process, complete with broadcast advertising, campaign billboards, direct mail, rallies, and all that sort of thing.

During this time period I worked in a number of rural, mostly bilingual Cherokee communities where we were facilitating projects ranging from housing to new water systems. In one small community, I came upon three of our people living in an abandoned bus. They looked like they were there

to stay. They had clothes hanging on a line and a wood-burning stove sitting outside. While this may have been an extreme case, I knew Cherokee people needed housing and other services. I suddenly understood that I was being given an opportunity to create change for Cherokee families such as those living in the old bus. I knew that if I did not act, I would no longer have any right to talk about or criticize the people who held tribal office. On that day, after visiting that community, I decided to seek election as deputy principal chief of the Cherokee Nation. I won the 1983 election, becoming the first woman to serve in that position, and in 1987 and in 1991 I was elected principal chief, also the first woman to serve in that position.

In 1995, after three elections, I decided not to seek election again. I felt my season at the Cherokee Nation had come to an end and it was time for new leadership to emerge. I have never regretted that decision, and though it has taken some time to happen, new leadership has indeed emerged. Now as I look forward to the new century, I am hopeful that one day soon our people will be able to live their lives on their own terms, just as I have.

Wilma Mankiller was the first woman ever elected principal chief of the Cherokee Nation.

A Diligent Student

ILEANA ROS-LEHTINEN

Born in Havana, Cuba, I came to the United States at the young age of seven, fleeing the persecution and violations that torment the Cuban people in the Castro regime. Even at seven years old, I was schooled in the ways in which Fidel Castro and his followers imposed their communist beliefs on the Cuban people, the way he stole and stripped Cubans of their every property and of their every right.

My family relocated to Miami, where my parents instructed me to study diligently to succeed in school. In college, I aspired to become an elementary school teacher, never realizing that this position would soon inspire me to hold public office.

After graduation, I began working in public elementary schools. I pursued my dream of providing children with a solid education for success by opening a small, private school named Eastern Academy, where I served as administrator and principal. As I went on with the work that running an elementary school commands, I realized I needed to shift gears and knock on the doors of the people who were in charge with developing educational standards in the state of Florida. As I began to lobby for laws to improve my state's educational system, I came to a big turning point in my career. I soon realized that the best way I could utilize my talents to improve the educational system in Florida was to devote my time and energy as a legislator in the Florida House of Representatives.

Serving as a state Representative and then as a state Senator, I implemented the successful and popular Florida Pre-Paid Tuition plan to expand access to

students seeking higher education. A special opportunity arose in 1989 as Congressman Claude Pepper passed away, leaving a vacant seat in the U.S. Congress. Although it was a difficult decision to make, I knew I could seize more opportunities to better serve my community as a U.S. Representative. Soon thereafter, I became the first Hispanic woman elected to Congress.

Because I came from an island whose people are deprived of all democratic human rights, I have worked tirelessly during my tenure in Congress to defend the inherent freedoms that should be granted to all peoples. I am most proud of the work I do to defend the cause of freedom, to defend those who cannot defend themselves, the subjugated, and those who have been silenced.

In 1998, I had the unique opportunity of being selected to represent the United States government at the funeral of Mother Teresa. The trip caused me to reflect upon the many ways in which she utilized her God-given talents to save children and people from death and starvation, to uplift their spirits, and to commit herself to a lifetime of giving without ever expecting anything in return. The ways in which Mother Teresa's lifetime of unselfish service have inspired me to give ear to and devote my efforts to my constituents have been countless.

The responsibilities of any American citizen are to take part in democracy and contribute to society by voting, by voicing their opinions, and by always taking into consideration what is good for all people of our country. As a naturalized citizen, I highly appreciate the liberties for which our forefathers fought and the rights that were granted us. Over the next decade, I hope to see these same freedoms restored to the Cuban people, from whom they were stripped, and democracy established in all oppressed nations.

Ileana Ros-Lehtinen, a Republican congresswoman from Florida, became in 1989 the first Hispanic woman elected to the United States Congress.

5 | Volunteer

America is a nation of volunteers. We volunteer for everything, and it is one of our best and most enduring traits. Alexis de Tocqueville, the Frenchman who came here in the 1820s and 1830s to study the U.S. political system, was astonished at how Americans got involved in a particular community problem. He said they would go across the street to a neighbor to talk about it and begin organizing. He had never seen this phenomenon in Europe. He wrote that the United States is run by volunteers, and in many ways he is correct.

Some argue that Americans are so busy these days that they have less and less time to volunteer for good causes. There's no question that we aren't getting enough good people into politics as volunteers or as candidates. But we don't see any dramatic drop-off in the willingness of most Americans to devote time to causes they believe in. The United States has more voluntary organizations than any other country of the world, and more are being created every day.

Some organizations, such as the Red Cross or the United Way, have been around for a long time and do great work. Almost every disease in the nation has an organization working and raising money for a cure. Our communities are full of good people working long hours as volunteers in local charitable and non-profit organizations to solve one problem or another.

Many of our cities and towns are covered with neighborhood associations, some of which have aged without declining and others that arose over a particular community problem. In one Boston neighborhood there are 19 neighborhood crime watch groups. Now that's volunteering!

And note how many of our contributing authors first began getting active in their communities through the causes they believed in. Former Oregon Governor Barbara Roberts, for example, could not find a school for her son disabled by autism. That got her into volunteering and ultimately into politics.

G etting involved in your community as a volunteer in a good cause is a great way to get to know people as well as your community. We suspect that many of you who read this are already volunteering in local efforts sponsored by religious and charitable groups.

We hope these experiences will encourage you to volunteer in politics as well, because volunteers really make the American political system tick. Yes, many campaigns are spending huge amounts of money—too much on television ads and on expensive campaign consultants. And, yes, the bigger the campaign and the district it covers, the more necessary it will be to put significant resources into television advertising, which is extremely expensive.

But we can tell you from our personal experiences that neither of us could have been elected dogcatcher without the thousands of hours that citizen volunteers devoted to our campaigns. In fact, we started as volunteers before we ran for public office. We licked stamps, stuffed envelopes, canvassed our neighborhoods, manned phone banks, and stood in front of supermarkets and factories pushing our candidates. (Always give the shopper or employee the literature on the way out, not on the way in. Managers do not take kindly to floors covered with discarded campaign literature.)

In communities with well-developed public transportation systems, bus or transit stops from seven to nine in the morning are great places for volunteers to promote their candidates. When Mike Dukakis first ran for the state legislature, he tried to determine where he and his volunteers could connect with voters on a Sunday before noontime. They ended up at the municipal golf course at five in the morning. You'd be amazed at the number of golf fanatics that are out there as the sun rises, waiting to tee off. Paul Simon found that after evening meetings, he and volunteers could go to bowling alleys and meet people who would rarely show up at a political event.

When Mike started running for state office, he and a crew of volunteers used to walk the beaches of Massachusetts in shorts and T-shirts for hours on summer Saturdays and Sundays, greeting people on beach blankets and supplying them with campaign literature. It was a great way to get a tan and a lot of votes, but he could never have done it without his weekend volunteers. These days people come up to Mike frequently to remind him that they first met him with those great young volunteers on the beaches north and south of Boston. Paul and his volunteers worked business areas in the same way.

What do volunteers do in a campaign? In a few words, just about everything. Why do they do it? Because they care about their community, state, and country, and they believe that the candidate they are working for is a person who reflects their beliefs and values and that, working for and through him or her, they can make an impact on the world around them—and because they find it an enjoyable experience.

As they spend more and more time as campaign volunteers, they begin to develop the skills that will make them valuable campaign workers. You may start by canvassing a small neighborhood. At first you probably will feel a bit awkward. You'll be amazed, however, at how interesting it can be and how receptive and friendly most people are to your knock on the door. And sometimes canvassing can be a real challenge. Mike remembers campaigning for the legislature door-to-door when the infamous Boston Strangler was on the loose, and people were frightened. Try to canvass under those circumstances! "Shove it under the door!" they would bellow. And so he would, at which point the voice on the other side would say "Wait a minute!" and then slowly, ever so slowly, the door would open a crack as they would peer out at him.

If, after doing your canvassing, you find that you have real organizational skills, you may be asked to take on responsibility for a full

precinct or a larger section of town or even become the field organizer for the campaign. That means recruiting other volunteers, training them, encouraging them to begin the process that you have already gone through, and making sure they are doing the neighborhoods that have been assigned to them.

Once you have proven yourself as a first-rate field organizer, you may be asked to manage a local campaign and take full responsibility for all aspects of the contest. When that happens, you will thank the day when you first volunteered, because that is when you first began to understand the political process, develop the necessary skills and appreciate what the volunteers that are now working for you as a manager are trying to do in their neighborhoods.

Let's suppose, however, that you are the type of person that doesn't particularly like to get involved in the organizational aspects of the campaign but cares deeply about policy and would like to work on issues. Don't despair. There is room for good policy people as volunteer researchers in virtually every campaign. Candidates have to address the issues. They must prepare for public forums and debates. They usually issue detailed position papers.

Most candidates care deeply about the issues. That is why they run for office. But they don't have the time to do all the research needed to help them develop their positions on all issues and back them up. They need people to do that kind of in-depth analysis, draft the position papers, go over the issues and alternatives with them, and help them prepare the speeches and press releases that a good candidate requires.

You can also volunteer after the campaign when the real business of government gets done. Both of us had the good fortune during our political careers to have the services of literally dozens of young interns who worked in our legislative or executive offices on a whole range of activities with which a busy senator or governor deals. Many received college or high school credit for their internships. They were generally required to do a paper at the end of their internship, supervised by senior staff in our offices. A high percentage of them are now in some form of public service, and many of our interns have run and won public office. In fact, one of the great joys of holding public office is the opportunity it gives you to open the door of public service to young interns and encourage and inspire them to get into politics themselves.

You don't have to wait for college. There is no reason many of you can't intern at the local level while still in high school. Ask your government teacher if it is possible for you to put together an internship that combines work in the classroom with actual experience at the local city or town hall or, if it is close enough, the state capitol. Mike had a series of interns during his legislative years who were high school seniors in their last semesters at the local high school. They worked a full semester for him and then made it their job to identify a junior who would be the "senior intern" the following year. They were terrific, and many of them ended up in politics and government after they graduated from college. One is now the senior *New York Times* correspondent in Istanbul, Turkey! A volunteer in one of Paul's campaigns is now the junior senator from Wisconsin, Senator Russ Feingold. Paul served in state government when an intern for Senator Paul Douglas impressed him. Later, when Simon became Lieutenant Governor of Illinois, he hired that intern. His name is Dick Durbin, now the senior U.S. Senator from Illinois.

When we tell you that volunteers play a critical role in the political process in this country, we mean it. It's also great for your resume. College admissions officers are uniformly impressed with high school seniors who have volunteered in campaigns or in the office of a public official. Best of all, you will meet some fine people who will become lifelong friends and, more than that, will be eager and able to help you shape your future. That may include a good recommendation for college. It almost certainly will mean a good friend who is more than willing to make the contact or phone call that will permit you to pursue your interest in public service.

Even though we both are no longer in elective office, we are asked all the time to write those recommendations and open up those doors,

and we do so enthusiastically. We have dedicated our lives to public service because we believe in it. We want others to follow in our footsteps and have the same opportunity to be of service. One of the reasons both of us teach now is because we want young people to appreciate just how exciting and rewarding public service is.

So take advantage of the opportunity to volunteer in politics and government. You won't regret it.

Fighting a Battle More Than Once

ELIZABETH DOLE

Women's role in politics has changed profoundly in the last half century. I can remember a time when the very idea of women as the equal of their male political counterparts seemed as unlikely as . . . well, the idea that a professional wrestler could be elected Governor of an American state.

Many of the questions we faced at the dawn of the women's "revolution" still remain—albeit in an updated '90s version.

For most women of my generation, we found the answers as we struggled individually to find our own identities. Although I pre-dated the "revolution," I was deeply involved in living it—sometimes consciously—more often, subconsciously. When we women knocked on the doors of America's law schools and medical and business schools in the '50s and early '60s, we were simply following our dreams, which seemed as natural to us as staying at home and getting married was to many others.

Still, there are many lessons to be learned from the past. When I was growing up, most women lived in a different America, a land barely recognizable to today's undergraduate. Back then, comparatively few women worked outside the home except as teachers, nurses, and secretaries. The government, whose original charter was written by 55 males in 18th century Philadelphia, placed women on a different plane as late as 1935, when Congress passed the National Recovery Act requiring that women working in government make at least 25 percent less than men in the same job. That was the year before I was born, and the world in which I was raised—in Salisbury, N.C., a wonderful, small, southern town that is still home to me today.

Few women in those days expected to work, and education for women was accordingly limited. It was rumored that no girl could hope to graduate from Boyden High School unless she could sew a button on or attach a zipper. Well, I did graduate, and the school yearbook predicted I would spend my life as a "French interpreter in an airport." They were half right. I do spend a lot of time in airports, but when I entered Duke University in the fall of 1954, instead of French, I chose political science as my major.

Life at Duke in the '50s bore little resemblance to college life today. Don't get me wrong. I loved Duke, but it was a far cry from college life today. As a freshman woman in 1954, I was given a handbook for academic success. A "Duchess" (yes, that's what they called us—Duchesses). Anyway, to succeed at Duke University, we "Duchesses" were told to eat breakfast every day, wear hats and hosiery to church, write thank-you notes to our dates, and avoid blue jeans.

It was a different world, but it was also a world in transition, even if we didn't realize it at the time. Women were beginning to question their traditional roles. Some of us weren't ready to accept the "place" that had been pre-ordained for us the moment the doctor told our mothers, "Congratulations. You have a beautiful little girl."

I was in the vanguard of change and wanted to take a different path. I have often thought back to that time in my life and wondered why. The answer is I don't honestly know why I listened to the beat of a different drummer, but I did. So, instead of settling down, I set out on a sabbatical to Oxford undertaken with my parents' worried blessing.

I don't know if it was the launch of the spacecraft *Sputnik* that spurred my interest in the Soviet Union or just the idea of going where few Americans

CONTINUED

had gone before, but while in England I got a hankering to visit the Soviet Union. Getting my parents' permission was almost as difficult as getting a visa.

I got my first real taste of politics during the summer of 1960, when I worked on Capitol Hill as a secretary in the office of North Carolina Senator Everett Jordan. That summer, I did one of the smartest things I've ever done—I sought out prominent women in government for professional guidance, one of whom changed my life. Senator Margaret Chase Smith, a Maine Republican, didn't know me from Adam, but she not only agreed to take time out of her busy schedule to see me, she gave me some of the best advice I've ever received.

Senator Smith urged me to get a law degree in order to bring more to a public policy job than just aptitude or a master's. Once asked what she believed to be the proper place for a woman, this wise Yankee lawmaker replied, "My answer is short and simple—a woman's proper place is every-where . . . if there is any proper place for women today," she said, "it is that of alert and responsible citizens in the fullest sense of the word."

Two years later, I entered Harvard Law School—much to the dismay of my mother and some of my classmates. Breaking the news to my parents wasn't easy. My mother asked me, "Don't you want to be a wife and a mother and a hostess for your husband?" I told her I wanted to be all of those things, but in my time. "Well," mother said, "your dad and I don't advise it, but it's your life, your little red wagon." They stood by me. But later that night, I was awakened by sounds of distress coming from the bathroom. Mother had lost her dinner. No doubt she thought she was also losing her daughter.

I can still vividly recall my first day of class. I was one of 24 women in a class of 550, but the very fact that I was there sitting in those tough classes competing with men meant that society was changing. Clearly, we had

managed to unlock the door, but we soon found out that no one was going to invite us in.

Sandra Day O'Connor, the first woman to serve on the Supreme Court, graduated third in her class from Stanford Law in 1952—no small feat—but was rejected for all associate's positions by every top law firm in California. She did finally get an offer from one Los Angeles firm—as a legal secretary.

Achievement in those days didn't necessarily translate into acceptance. Justice O'Connor, who is also a wife, mother, and former state legislator, has said that without the women's movement, she would have never been appointed to the Court. In the '50s and early '60s, women like Justice O'Connor were the quiet revolutionaries—the front-line troops before the main assault force hit the beaches in the late '60s.

But by the time I left Harvard in 1965, women were turning what had often been lonely, individual struggles into an emerging national movement. For the first time, we were beginning to define our roles in society for ourselves.

I remember the day in the early 1970s when I was working at the Nixon White House as Deputy Special Assistant to the President for Consumer Affairs, and I hurried to the Metropolitan Club in Washington for a meeting with some Cleveland, Ohio, attorneys and businessmen.

As I rushed by the doorman, he yelled, "Stop! You can't go in there, lady! Women are not permitted in this club!" I told him there must be some misunderstanding. "My name is Elizabeth Hanford," I said. "I work at the White House, and I have a meeting on the fourth floor with some businessmen who have flown in from Cleveland."

"I'm sorry," he said. "If you were Queen Elizabeth, you still couldn't go in."

CONTINUED

That was then. This is now. Today, more than 40 percent of the students entering Harvard Law School are women. I can recommend from first hand experience the Caesar salad at the Metropolitan Club. And, when I was Secretary of Labor, I met regularly with seven Assistant Secretaries, and four of them—for Policy, Congressional Affairs, Public Affairs, and International Affairs—were women and, I might add, paid the same as men.

Women have now served in most Cabinet posts, and we have our first woman Secretary of State and Attorney General. And, I am proud to say that last year the Republican conference elected the first woman majority leader in history, Jennifer Dunn of Washington. What a huge step forward for all these women—in fact, for all Americans. All of these women are in their positions today because they are eminently qualified, but also because women have become a political force that cannot be ignored.

The '70s and '80s brought enormous change for women here at home and around the world. In Britain, where tradition is as sacrosanct as football, Margaret Thatcher upset the status quo and inspired women the world over. When the Thatchers moved to 10 Downing Street, a reporter asked Denis Thatcher, the Prime Minister's husband, who wore the pants in his house?

Mr. Thatcher, ever good-natured, answered, "I do, and I also wash them and iron them." I guess you could say Denis Thatcher, too, broke down centuries of tradition, thereby paving the way for a whole new generation of men to come.

For those of us who can remember "then," believe me, we are grateful that it is "now." That even includes my mother, still my best friend and still living independently in her house in Salisbury—a very modern traditionalist. Indeed, I think that most of the women she grew up with would have, in time, embraced their new roles and opportunities—and for good reason.

In their day, women rarely attended college, could not vote or realistically expect to hold office or otherwise influence a public debate. If married, they had no rights to sue, divorce, or own property. Today, almost eight million women own businesses that generate an amazing $2.3 trillion in sales a year. Women-owned businesses employ one out of every four workers in the United States today.

The calendar says it's 2000. Until women equal their male counterparts in earnings and managerial opportunities, our work remains unfinished. Fortunately, time and technology are on our side.

There is abundant evidence that women will be called upon to assume leadership roles in coping with the revolutionary changes now affecting America's workforce. The future is our friend.

In politics, the rise of women has been just as remarkable. Women are becoming leaders themselves in greater and greater numbers. It didn't happen overnight, and it was a circuitous route for many.

In 1978, when I was serving on the Federal Trade Commission, 46 women ran for the U.S. House—16 were successful. In 1998, 121 women entered the fray, and 56 of them took the oath of office. At the same time, nine women followed in the steps of Margaret Chase Smith as they entered the U.S. Senate.

But this isn't just a Washington phenomenon. Across the country, women are making gains in elective office at every level. Over the past 30 years, the number of women serving in the state legislature has increased more than fivefold. Many of these women are positioned to move on to higher office.

In 1998, the state of Arizona voted itself into a league all its own. Although there has been relatively scant media coverage, Arizona voters chose women

CONTINUED

for all five top constitutional offices—Governor, Secretary of State, Attorney General, State Treasurer, and Superintendent of Public Instruction. That, in and of itself, is a pretty remarkable statement about just how far we've come.

To be sure, women care just as much about tax cuts and national defense as any man, but women have changed the issue mix both as candidates and as voters. As they have gained power from the boardroom to the ballot box, elected leaders—of both sexes—have embraced a new, broader set of issues. We certainly saw it in the congressional elections in 1998 as the emphasis shifted to such "kitchen table" priorities as health care, education, and the future of Social Security.

That women in politics are a force to be reckoned with should be self-evident. But why is this? In fact, more women than men have voted in every election since at least 1964—when turnout by gender was first recorded. It's a fact that has not gone unnoticed by the pundits, the political consultants, or the candidates. And winning campaigns make the women's vote a part of candidates' strategy.

Young women today have a vastly greater range of choices than we did. No longer are they restricted by the stereotyping that characterized my mother's generation and lingered on into my own. Nor are they limited by the short-sighted, self-imposed demands of the '60s and '70s that a woman choose a career in order to validate her existence.

Today, you can be you—whatever that means. As the pendulum swings, I believe it will finally rest wisely in the center where women may choose a career or family or both. There is a price to pay for such choices, but that knowledge is part of our progress. Or perhaps I should say we, like America itself, are a work in progress. Women still face discrimination, but the

remaining inequalities we face will never be erased without great political participation by women at every level.

Meanwhile, I worry frankly that as we find our "proper place," we will confront other problems both as new and as old as womanhood itself. For the past 30 years women have had to be overachievers to succeed, to work twice as hard as men to be considered half as good.

Unfortunately, that hasn't changed entirely, and as Margaret Thatcher says, "You may have to fight a battle more than once to win it."

At the same time, while men have become more involved in the home, the traditional role for most women remains that of nurturer—nothing wrong with that. But the constant pressure for perfectionism, to be the super executive or the supermom or both, inevitably takes a toll.

How will success be defined for women of the next generation? I suspect somewhat differently than for women of mine or even for those making their choices today. Women of my generation and the one that followed were told not that we could do anything, but that we could do everything . . . a career . . . a marriage . . . a family . . . serve as a volunteer. And still have time for ourselves and our souls—all without compromise.

I have no real regrets, but I do wish someone, once upon a time, had told me that I had to choose. Because some choices should be made consciously, with open eyes. So, as a woman with some years of perspective, I hope you will indulge me a few observations on the state of women today and maybe just a little advice. We now know that not everything we were told was true. Even in our crowded lives—especially in our crowded lives—we have to make choices. We can't have it all. Time and energy and the realities of life

CONTINUED

will not allow it. Our modern freedom to choose requires us to decide among our wants. We must decide what is important, what is lasting, what is noble.

I know so many women today who have come to this point of reflection. As they balance the demands of work and family, they struggle to steady their personal lives—to bring a wholeness to their existence that might otherwise go missing.

In our frenzied lives, when the sheer pace and volume of modern existence sometimes seems to overwhelm our essential humanity, this much seems clear—as human beings, women have spiritual needs that match or exceed those for worldly accomplishments.

As I was preparing for my duties as president of the American Red Cross, my mother reminded me that she had once served as a Red Cross volunteer during World War II. And she said, "Elizabeth, nothing I ever did made me feel so important."

Perhaps in the final analysis that is what success is all about—finding something which infused you with a sense of mission, with a passion for your life's work; finding something that leads you to say, "nothing I ever did made me feel so important."

Across America are those who've discovered that feeling through a career as a businesswoman, a volunteer, a professor, a public servant, and a mother. No one can tell you where you will find that feeling—how you will define success—that's a decision we must make for ourselves.

I don't believe there is one path for women or one nature to fulfill. Real fulfillment is often different than we imagine and better than we plan. And that's when we say to ourselves, "This is it. This is real. The rest is just decoration."

It may mean giving up some things; but in moments like those, it doesn't take real sacrifice. It feels like coming home. We rediscover the life we almost lost in the living.

For many, public service can help provide the pathway home to true fulfillment for anyone who professes a deeper commitment to others. To me, this is yet another step in the evolution of American womanhood. We benefited enormously from the Civil Rights Act of 1964. We have grown increasingly comfortable with the reins of power. Now, we must accept the social responsibility that goes with the power.

So what, you ask, is a woman's place in the next millennium? It is, in fact, anywhere she wants to be, and anywhere her conscience directs her: On the ballot or chauffeuring little girls to ballet class; leading a Senate Committee or helping a young man learn to read; sitting in the Oval Office or sitting on the Court of Appeals or sitting with a sick child in the night.

We've come a long way from then to now. From the fight for suffrage to nine senators, 54 members of the House, two Supreme Court Justices, 22 Cabinet members, and a Majority Leader—we have traveled a historic route, and the journey is far from over.

Whenever the next generation of women seeks to build on the work of their predecessors, they demonstrate the wisdom of Emerson's assertion that: "A sufficient measure of civilization is the influence of good women."

Elizabeth Dole, former president of the American Red Cross (1991 to 1999), has served five U.S. Presidents in various positions and ran in 1999 to become the Republican nominee for President of the United States.

6 | Concentrate on One or Two Issues

Every holder of public office receives letters from well intentioned people who write at great length and tell you their positions on 27 issues. They should save their postage. Writing about 27 issues is the equivalent of writing on none. Officeholders and their staffs are not likely to be impressed.

It is fairly common for candidates to make the same mistake, to spread themselves too thin, and to speak on everything. The effect on the public is the same as the letter writer who sermonizes on 27 issues. As a candidate, you have to answer questions from reporters on where you stand on key issues. You should not duck taking a stand. But the candidate's speeches and advertisements should be focused on one or two political issues that really concern him or her.

We suggest that even now during your school days, while you absorb as much knowledge as you can in many areas, it would be wise to pick one or two issues that really interest you and concentrate your efforts on those one or two.

As you become more and more familiar with one or two issues, the word will spread. People will be impressed that you know so much about a particular subject. And you will discover how the political process works on issues. By being informed, you have a greater chance to make a contribution to a better society. A year from now other

issues may interest you more than the one or two you select today. But the background acquired will benefit you for the rest of your life.

W hat should that one issue or those two issues be? You probably have an idea already. Reading a newspaper or news magazine should generate some thoughts. But here are some additional ideas—not even one percent of the possibilities:

—Discouraging Teenage Smoking

—Mental Health

—Adult Illiteracy

—The Prison System: What Are the Alternatives?

—Poverty Among U.S. Children

—The Coming World Water Crisis: What Should We Do?

—The U.S. Falling Behind Other Nations in Foreign Language Instruction

—Affirmative Action

—Finding Jobs for the Hard to Employ

—Taxes: Are They Fair?

—Status of Our National Parks

—Urban Mass Transit: Do We Want to Save It?

—Amtrak: How Will We Pay For It?

—Aid to Africa: How Do We Generate Interest?

—Health Care

—Campaign Financing

—Pre-School Education

—Drug Addiction

—Reducing the Crime Rate

—Reducing Violence in Schools

You can add to that list, but pick only one or two topics. Read about that issue or issues. Write to your state and national legislators for background information. Ask their opinions. If you follow through on whatever topic you select, within a matter of weeks you may become the most knowledgeable person in your community on that specific subject.

When you feel on top of the issue enough to believe that a certain course should be followed by the state or national government or by your local city council or county board, then write to those officials or talk to them. Keep a careful record of whom you have contacted and what their responses are.

Your library should be helpful on the issues. The Internet can give you some leads on your topic.

Once you have an issue or two selected, talk to people who might be knowledgeable. They can give you tips. It is important to try to stick to one or two basic messages. If you try to make a speech or issue a press release each day on whatever is on the front page of the news-papers that day, you will generate attention, but people will soon lose sight of your core issues. As a candidate, you may tire of giving much the same speech over and over and over, but as you repeat it, and adapt it to the local situation, you will gradually reach more and more people with the basic message. Office-seekers often feel like they are repeating a message constantly, but for most listeners it will be new. Getting a message on an issue across to people in a local race—or a state or national race—is not easy. Teachers are told, "You have to repeat over and over and over to get a point across to students." The same is true for candidates and the public.

W hen you become a candidate, you must be realistic and stress the issues that you think are important, but that are also popular. For example, the two of us—Paul Simon and Michael Dukakis—oppose capital punishment. It is a punishment we reserve for people of limited means, and there is no evidence that it retards crime. Western Europe, Canada, and Mexico have abandoned it. But the position the two of us take is not popular. Polls show that overwhelmingly the American people favor capital punishment. So when we made television campaign commercials, we did not stress this unpopular stance but other positions that had greater general appeal.

However, an issue you select for emphasis should be something in which you really believe. If you simply follow the polls and try to pick a popular issue, but one you really don't care about, the people with whom you speak are likely to sense that conviction is lacking. Conviction is something people want in leaders, even though the public sometimes makes mistakes in determining who has it.

When you have an issue or issues selected, write one or two pages on each one to set out your basic thoughts at the time. Then put that aside in a drawer while you read more about it, and talk to your friends to get their ideas. Make notes while you have their thoughts fresh in your mind. Have a folder or notebook at home where you keep the information you are getting. After you have worked on this a few weeks, get that paper you put aside, and read it again. Probably your views will have changed a little.

It is possible you can use some of this material for a term paper in school, but if that cannot be done, you will nevertheless have enriched yourself with more knowledge and helped to prepare yourself for the day when you may become a candidate.

Champion of a Cause

BARBARA ROBERTS

I have a place in Oregon history and a place in the history of our country—I was elected as the first woman Governor in Oregon and became one of the first 10 elected women Governors in America.

This statement sounds pretty impressive and it might lead you to believe there is something special and unique about a woman who makes history. But, in truth, each of us is only one cause, one tragedy, one concern, one moral indignation away from active political involvement. The cause that stirs you may be just around the corner.

I began my political career as a citizen advocate, a parent, seeking educational rights for my autistic son. My older son had been sent home from school in the first grade—not for the day but forever. His disability meant he had no right to a public school education. And I could not appeal—not to the school board, the courthouse, or the state house. The law gave my son no recognition, no rights, no recourse. But I simply could not accept the unfairness, the inequity, the fact that my son's disability would be exacerbated by his also being uneducated. I spoke out publicly about the injustice. I pleaded for help. I sought a hero. I waited for a leader to step forward to champion our children's cause. By the end of the 1960s, I was a divorced mother with two sons, no child support, and a low-paying office job. But I was unwilling, any longer, to let those liabilities short-change my son. I finally came to recognize I had two crucial assets: a cause and a mother's anger! If I could not find the leader I sought, I would assume that position by self-appointment.

So, I took a day a week off work (and the painful related pay cut), traveled to my state capitol, and began a fight for my son's educational rights. I was politically inexperienced, scared to death, and didn't have the money to buy so much as a cup of coffee for a state legislator. But I marched up the capitol steps determined to change the world for the disabled children of my state.

Five months later Oregon had the first law in the nation requiring public education for children like my son. It was not until five years later that a federal law passed, granting such rights to disabled children in all 50 states.

I had moved the mountain of government. I had made a difference for hundreds of Oregon children. That first political success for my son cemented my belief that, if your cause is just, you are determined enough, and you can make your case well enough—one person can make a difference in the political process. I learned it then; I believe it still.

That experience also taught me that silence is not golden on the issues of equity, fairness, civil and human rights, and inclusion. Without individuals willing to stand up and speak out, unfairness will always continue. And, in most cases, to make a real difference, those stands must be taken in the political process.

My son's life was changed dramatically by my first political efforts. But, just as dramatic were the changes it brought to my life and, eventually, to my state's history. Soon after that legislative session, I ran for and was elected to my local school board. Next, was a four-year term as an elected community college board member. Those two successful elections made me a viable candidate for appointment to fill a one-year vacancy on the county commission. Suddenly, this struggling young mom was holding paid political office in the most populous county in Oregon!

CONTINUED

From the county commission I ran successfully for the Oregon House of Representatives, becoming my state's first woman House Majority Leader in only my second term as a state representative.

In a decade, I had moved from a volunteer citizen advocate to House Majority Leader. But those elections and my titles weren't nearly so important as the reinforcement they gave to my strong belief that one person could make a difference in the political process and, in turn, a difference for people.

On the school board, my leadership and my vote helped start the kindergarten program. I was part of the team that created a highly effective displaced worker program at our community college. As County Commissioner, I cast one of the deciding votes to build Portland's impressive light rail system. In the legislature, I became a strong advocate for education funding, environmental protection, alcohol and drug treatment, and overhauling Oregon's juvenile justice system. Year by year, vote by vote, I was making a difference in programs serving thousands of my state's citizens. I was also gaining knowledge and expertise on a breadth of issues, from taxation to land use, from adoption to forestry, from election law to economic development policy.

In 1983, I was faced with a major political and personal decision. Should I or should I not run for statewide political office? The Secretary of State's term was ending, and I didn't see a member of my own political party who seemed prepared to take on the challenge. It reminded me of my search for someone to help Oregon's disabled children receive their rightful education. If I couldn't find the candidate I sought, I needed to step forward myself and assume that leadership role. And I did!

In November of 1984, I was elected Oregon's first Democratic Secretary of State in 110 years! That win took a year of hard work, total commitment, and

tough fundraising efforts. In Oregon, the Secretary of State also holds the positions of Lieutenant Governor and State Auditor. When you win the position, it is considered a stepping stone to the governorship. But, for me, I felt I had reached my political pinnacle. I couldn't yet see myself as Oregon's Governor.

I was reelected Secretary of State in 1988, winning all 36 counties in the state. During those years I spoke constantly to groups of citizens of all stripes throughout Oregon, bringing state government and policy issues directly to our citizens. I loved my work and the role of interacting with Oregonians. I felt privileged to be a statewide elected official. My family had come to Oregon on the Oregon Trail. Now I was pioneering ideas—and women's leadership—in this state of my ancestors.

In early 1990 the incumbent Governor, a member of my political party, withdrew from his reelection bid, creating a shock in Oregon political circles and a late vacancy in the nomination process. The next day I announced as a candidate for Governor! No one believed I had a prayer of winning with such a last-minute campaign, no money raised, and no organization in place. But it wasn't the first time I'd been a "long shot" in that capitol building or in my political career. It wasn't the first time I'd watched doubters smile and friends had patted me on the head like a good child. Yet against all odds and the predictions of the press and pundits, eight months later I became the first woman Governor in Oregon history.

Few people in Oregon would disagree that the Oregon governorship between 1991 and 1995 was one of the toughest tenures in my state's history. Oregon was right at the height of the spotted owl/timber crisis, an angry, polarizing debate between the environment and the economy. Oregon citizens had just passed the most restrictive tax limitation law in the state's history. Oregon was experiencing a notable population explosion. Plus, like the rest

CONTINUED

Champion of a Cause CONTINUED

of the nation, we were in the midst of the most anti-government period in modern history.

Being Oregon's Governor was a tough job—a very tough job—but someone had to do it. And I've never regretted being there in the tough time. It is, in fact, in these challenging times of transition that leadership matters most. So for those hectic and challenging years I served as Governor, I came to believe strongly in risk taking, in building scar tissue, and in taking the road less traveled. Without the courage to risk it all for the common good, there can be no true leadership.

In my four years as Governor I was often described as the strongest environmental Governor in the nation. When I finished my four-year term, Oregon had the lowest unemployment in 25 years and the highest investment in the state's history. I was a recognized government "reinventer" and a national and state leader for human and civil rights. It is a record I carry with pride. Oregon is a different and, I believe, better place because I traveled the road of political leader. I have been honored to call myself a politician.

Barbara Roberts was elected the first woman Governor of Oregon in 1991.

 Personal Political Narratives

Governing with a Vision

STEPHEN GOLDSMITH

On a daily basis, as Mayor of Indianapolis, Indiana, I have the opportunity to interact with a diverse array of people, but none that I treasure more than our city's young people. While many question the drive and activism of our nation's youth, I have found that not only are our young people bright and energetic, they are often the most civic-minded citizens we have. That is why I value this opportunity to join other political leaders in encouraging your participation in the American political process.

At the heart of our political system is the basic desire to improve the quality of life for all of our citizens. There are numerous contributions one can make toward that goal, but none more productive or direct than participating in government and politics.

Like many of you, I began my participation in political life during high school, simply motivated to make my school a better place and the community around it more successful. While I did become actively involved in student government, running for student council president and class officer, I also participated in community-service clubs, one of the easiest and most important ways to get involved in public life.

Through those experiences I learned that public service has a broad definition. While political office often receives the most attention, helping others run for office or developing and advocating public policies are also meaningful ways to become involved in your community. That is why today, with such a severe shortage of talented individuals willing to invest time and energy in public service, there is a role for any principled, conscientious person who is willing to get involved.

CONTINUED

Governing with a Vision CONTINUED

My continued involvement in student government and community service organizations in college helped me learn a valuable lesson that I later used in my campaign for public office. It is important, before you become involved in any activity, to stake out what you intend to accomplish through your participation. If you want to run for office or join an organization simply to earn a title or gain power, then it is probably not worthwhile and will lead to expending much energy without valuable results. Adding principle to effort will make your participation more honorable and, in the end, more successful as well.

After finishing law school, I saw a dramatic need, not only in Indianapolis, but across the country, to make our streets safer for law-abiding citizens. That is why I decided to run for my first public office, Prosecuting Attorney of Marion County, Indiana. I was prosecutor for more than 10 years, during which time I developed strong relationships with many Indianapolis residents and became intrigued by issues that extended beyond public safety.

That is why, in the fall of 1991, I decided to run for Mayor of Indianapolis and was reelected in 1995. As Mayor, I have been able to address a wide range of issues that affect the quality of the lives of our residents. During my tenure as Mayor, Indianapolis has developed a reputation as a highly successful city with a smaller, more efficient government. In order to achieve that success, we sought to incorporate many nontraditional organizations into our city government. As a result, many community groups and faith-based institutions have been given the authority and resources to solve some of our city's most troubling social problems. In order to forge these community coalitions, I had to reach across racial, religious, and even partisan lines, alienating some members in my own party. Yet I feel strongly that building broad-based coalitions is one of the crucial components to success in public life.

As I complete my final year as Mayor and look ahead to my future involvement in public life, I am increasingly concerned about the fragmented nature of our communities. The mandate to heal those divisions will fall upon our next generation of political leaders. Your future involvement is essential to ensure that we create a civil society of citizens who have an active stake in our communities and who are mobilized to pursue productive careers in public service.

Stephen Goldsmith was elected in November 1991 as Mayor of Indianapolis, the nation's 12th largest city.

7 | Expand Your Circle of Experience— and Friends

B oth of us have been in and around politics for a long time. Looking back on our high school and college days, we certainly didn't lead sheltered lives. But most of us tend to live, go to school, and work in roughly the same circle. We associate with people like ourselves, and only occasionally do we break out of our normal routine. Politics changes all that. It will provide you with knowledge and experiences that you would otherwise never get, and we guarantee you will meet and make some of the best friends you have ever had.

So if you are interested in getting involved politically, you should make a point of getting out into your community and begin to connect with people outside your normal circle of life. If you are Greek Orthodox or Lutheran, as we are, and there is a special event at a local synagogue, Catholic church, or mosque, attend it. Perhaps you don't have a religious affiliation and are interested in learning more about the people of various faiths in your community. Stick around after the event and meet some of the people who are there. Ask questions— good questions—about what you have just seen or heard. Get to know the people who are responsible for the event.

When a local ethnic group has a picnic or a festival, drop in on it. Chat with the people behind the serving tables. Eat the ethnic food. Watch the ethnic dancers. Do a little dancing yourself.

Have you even been to a Greek festival? They generally run the entire weekend at the local Greek Orthodox parish. Eat lamb on a stick and some baklava. Watch the Greek line dancing. Jump into the line, and see if you can master the simple steps of the hasapiko. It looks more difficult than it is, and if you learn it, the local Greek-Americans will love you for it. Mike remembers the time he took Kitty to her first Greek picnic. She was a modern dancer, and she had taught modern dancing. She watched the Greek dances for about five minutes, jumped into the line, and was leading it by the time the dance was over. People loved her for it.

What about a Polish picnic? Is there anything better than a kielbasa sausage on a crisp autumn afternoon? And you'll develop the ability to dance the polka in ways that you never knew were in you.

Have you ever been to an African-American gospel service on a Sunday morning? If you haven't, go. It is one of the great experiences of life. You will be struck, as we were, by the way the congregation is deeply and actively involved in the service and how politics and faith are woven together in the preacher's sermon. Both of us have been invited to speak to those congregations, and we have never come away from them without a new and better understanding of the range and richness of religious expression in this country.

We felt the same way when we attended a mariachi mass at a Mexican-American Roman Catholic church. Literally thousands of parishioners were packed into the church and singing hymns in Spanish with faith and gusto to the wonderful sounds and tempo of a mariachi band.

Both of us come from a rich ethnic and religious background. But if it hadn't been for politics, we would have hardly known our communities and our country.

Don't ignore civic and fraternal groups in and around your community. Join the Rotary or Kiwanis or Lions; affiliate with the local woman's club or chapter of the American Association of University Women. Drop in on a Chamber of Commerce forum. If a local union has an open meeting, make it a point to be there. If the Red Cross needs volunteers for a disaster in a neighboring community, become a volunteer. Donate blood. And as you make the rounds, introduce yourself. Get to know some of the people you meet. Make a list of their names and addresses. It will come in handy someday.

When we first ran for public office, we sat down with voting lists and systematically went through them from beginning to end, looking for the names of people we knew, people we had met, people whose children had gone to school with us, people who knew our parents.

They all received a letter announcing our candidacy and asking for their help. And many of them responded either because they knew our families or because we got to know them in the course of our visits to community and religious events.

But be genuine about what you are doing, and take a real interest in different people and their organizations. People can spot a phony. But they will appreciate the fact that you are really interested in them and their activities, and you will be surprised at how many of them will respond to an appeal for help if and when you decide to throw your "hat in the ring."

Above all, train yourself to be a good listener. Most people don't listen well, and we include ourselves when we first started out on our long political journeys. We were so full of energy and so committed to our causes that we wanted to talk about them all the time and assumed that people wanted to hear what we had to say about the great issues of the day. They sometimes do, but they also want the opportunity to share with you their ideas, their background, their ethnic and cultural heritage, and their pride in their families and communities.

You will miss a lot if you don't listen well. How do you become a good listener? By having a genuine interest in others and what they

have to say. Ask questions of others. All of us like to talk about ourselves. Give them that opportunity, and you will learn from them if you listen. Follow up if they ask you to pursue an issue or some concern for them. Make sure you and your volunteers never say you will try to do something about a concern and then not do it. It may mean calling the constituents back to say that you have tried and can't seem to get them the result they want. Ninety-nine times out of a hundred, they will appreciate the fact that you tried.

Former Florida Governor and now U.S. Senator Bob Graham has an interesting way of making sure that happens. He always carries a small three-by-five-inch spiral notebook in his inside breast pocket, and he writes everything down. Graham now has thousands of these pads full of notes and reminders to himself, but the fact that he has never lost a statewide election in Florida testifies to how effective it is.

Graham does something else that has become his trademark. He works a full day at a different occupation on a regular basis, and he has been doing so ever since he ran for Governor. One day he may work as a baggage handler at the Miami International Airport. Another it may be teaching a full school day at a local Florida high school. If you ask him, he will tell you it isn't just a campaign gimmick; he learns more about the people he is trying to represent during those work days than in any other thing he does. The people with whom he works never forget the fact that this two-term Governor and now three-term U.S. Senator spent a full day working alongside them, sharing their work and their ideas. And Bob Graham is one of the best listeners we know.

Both of us have had the experience of coming home after an 18-hour campaign day bone-tired but thoroughly exhilarated by the experiences we have had during a full day on the campaign trail. Why? Because you learn so much and because your faith in the American people is reinforced by being out there with them in their homes and in their communities.

There is no country in the world with the richness and variety of this one. Politics helps you to appreciate that in ways that simply can't be found in any other walk of life.

Personal Political Narratives

Reflections on a Life of Public Service

BY MARK O. HATFIELD

At the tender age of 10, my first taste of the political arena was one of bitter defeat. Though my mother and father were of different political persuasions— one being Democrat and the other Republican—both were Prohibitionists and supported the incumbent, Mr. Hoover. So, in 1932, I took a Republican stand and campaigned door-to-door in my hometown of Salem, Oregon, pulling behind me a little red wagon full of "Re-Elect Hoover" flyers. President Hoover's defeat came as a blow.

My own foray into public service was more successful. As a young political science professor at my alma mater, Willamette University, I made the decision to run for the state House of Representatives. With the university administration giving the blessing, it seemed feasible to be able to teach early classes and make it to the ten o'clock legislative sessions at the state capitol, just across the street from the campus. The constituents of my district chose me from among a field of 12 Republican candidates, and a 46-year career in politics was launched.

Thinking back to that first campaign brings to mind some of the basic elements that are foundational to political life. First and foremost is cultivating personal relationships. My basic philosophy of political life is building relationships with individuals by learning about and serving their needs. In other words, the bottom line is people. One way to build these relationships is through involvement in causes and issues that are of great interest to you. Volunteer experiences provide a tremendous learning forum and an ideal way to meet and work with a variety of citizens.

Along the way, I have been blessed to cross paths with people from every walk of life who have impacted my thinking and my life's work. Most have

names you would not recognize, but a great many notables are among that number, as well. I view my friendship with Mother Teresa as among the most significant. She helped me to see the needs of the poor and disenfranchised as through the eyes of Christ, and I will never forget walking alongside her in the streets and orphanages of Calcutta.

With election to office comes the mantle of leadership. Those with whom you have worked, and to whom you have made commitments, expect and deserve a public servant who not only serves but endeavors to be a leader rather than a follower of fickle polls. It is no easy task, but an elected official has the responsibility of both blending and creating public opinion. Decisions must be made not based on short-term gratification, but on problem solving with a view to long-term effects.

Many of the major issues facing our nation today could easily be identified as spiritual questions. For instance, environmental concerns are essentially issues of proper stewardship of land and resources. The problem of achieving economic equity might be looked at as an outgrowth of selfishness and greed, which create economic imbalances, lessening the full impact of human dreams and endeavors.

This viewpoint is not an attempt to put government in the business of dispensing religion because, as with all great spiritual awakenings, change must emanate from the hearts and minds of individual citizens. My call on all citizens is to wish and pray—and take steps to achieve—a spiritual renaissance for our nation so that human potential can be maximized.

Mark O. Hatfield, former Governor of Oregon, served for many years in the United States Senate as a Republican.

Going into Politics

PATSY T. MINK

When I returned to Hawaii from law school in 1952, Hawaii was in the midst of political turmoil. We had been annexed as a territory of the United States in 1898, and since that time had been ruled from Washington, DC. In the early 1950s, that meant that the Republican Party controlled all levels of government in the territory, as the Governor was appointed by the President.

Fervor for change was intense and widespread. The return of Japanese American veterans from World War II contributed enormously to the fervor. Many of these veterans returned not only from war, but also from college, for the GI Bill had given them an opportunity for higher education by underwriting their tuition and paying them a stipend.

For all veterans and for graduates of mainland colleges and professional schools, returning to Hawaii meant having to change it. We could not settle back into the racial and economic hierarchy; we could not compromise our ambitions and our dignity.

We needed to change the way we were governed. Winning such change fueled the rise of the new Democratic Party, of which I became a member. We demanded changes in tax policies so that landowners had to pay their fair share. We demanded changes in landownership so that ordinary people could acquire homes. We demanded more support for public

education so that students could go on to higher education. We called for a people's democracy.

Very quickly, I became one of the leading Democratic Party activists working for change. 1954 was the first year that Democratic majorities were elected to the Hawaii Territorial Legislature. I worked as a staff attorney that session in the House of Representatives. In 1956, I decided that I was ready to run for office. I stunned everyone with a spectacular victory, garnering the most votes in a multi-member district race.

MAKING A DIFFERENCE

I am most proud of the amendment that I worked to add to the Education Amendments in 1972, now referred to as "Title IX." Not only did I help win Title IX in 1972, but when it came under attack in 1975, I led the fight to preserve it. Title IX has transformed educational opportunities for girls and women throughout the country and in all levels of schooling. It has opened up all areas of academic pursuit to women, has made sure that women have equal access to educational funding, and has given girls and women the opportunity to develop into world-class athletes. The victorious 1999 U.S. women's soccer team credits Title IX for having opened the doors to their success.

SERVING IN POLITICAL OFFICE

Electing someone to public office is the highest honor that a democratic society can bestow on her. It represents the voters' grant of trust and authority to an individual to make decisions on their behalf. It is not only an honor, however; it also is an awesome responsibility that carries with it a

CONTINUED

tremendous obligation to act with integrity and with respect both for the office and for the people.

As a legislator, I have been entrusted by my constituents to develop the policies that will govern them. I may draft legislation, fight for proposals I support, and oversee the implementation of the laws by the various agencies of the executive branch.

Besides voting on legislation and speaking out on issues, an elected official helps her or his constituents with their individual problems with the government. Helping citizens navigate the bureaucracy is one of my most challenging tasks.

BEING A CITIZEN

Being a citizen in a democracy means that you have the power and the duty to help create the kind of government and society you want to live in.

To meet your duty, you must first be a registered voter and then must take voting in elections seriously. Democracy means collective self-government, and that means that we all must participate in the political process.

We do not fulfill our duty to participate merely by voting, however. We must be engaged and active members of the polity, ready to contribute at every opportunity. This includes expressing our opinions in appropriate forums, whether before government, in newspapers, or on the street corners. A democracy in which the majority is silent most of the time quickly becomes a democracy for the few.

LOOKING AHEAD

The most important task ahead for America is to improve public education at all levels. A poorly educated America will not be a politically robust America. A poorly educated America will not prosper amid world competition. For the sake of the future citizenry, the future of our democracy, and for the sake of all Americans' economic opportunity and material welfare, we must make education our highest priority.

Patsy Takemoto Mink, a Democrat Congresswoman in the United States House of Representatives from 1965 to 1977 and from 1991 to the present, is a member of the House Education and Workforce and Government Reform committees.

8 | Become More Visible

The prosecuting attorney in Madison County, Illinois, is William Haine, widely respected for being both honest and capable. Political leaders in that county first learned about Bill Haine when he was a high school student in Alton, Illinois, and volunteered to help in a campaign. He made a favorable impression on many people, and they learned he didn't just talk about things that needed to be done, he did them.

Penny Severns, as a high school student in Decatur, Illinois, volunteered in campaigns and became known in a small circle as being effective. As a young woman she won election to the Decatur City Council, later became a State Senator and then a candidate for Lieutenant Governor of Illinois. She traveled the state talking about important issues, knowing that if she did that the state would benefit from her campaign whether she won her election or not. She lost. A few years later she died of breast cancer, at the age of 46. She did not live to the traditional "ripe old age," but she filled her 46 years with more activity and contributions than most people do in a much longer life span. But Penny started when she was a high school student.

Bill and Penny are examples of people who got political experience early, and in the process made themselves favorably known to leaders. Those of us who hold public office or offices within our political parties know that people who "talk a good game" outnumber the people who actually get out and do the work. These two young people

became favorably known by political activists, but more than 95 percent of the population of their counties had never heard of either one. But those who knew the two of them learned quickly that they were not just talkers.

Bill and Penny are not typical. Both of us were interested in politics and issues when we attended high school, and were involved in student government, but we did not become active in the way that Bill Haine and Penny Severns did. What is true of the two of us is true of most people in political life. However, early involvement is helpful, both to understand the issues and the process and to become visible in a positive way to those who are political leaders and could help an aspiring young candidate.

We mention becoming visible "in a positive way." Getting arrested for driving under the influence of alcohol gives you visibility but does not aid a political career. Self-discipline in personal conduct is helpful in any field, particularly one in which you "live in a fishbowl," such as political life, when almost anything can be criticized.

It is not only personal conduct that should be watched. If you become visible on some issue, learn to understand both sides of the controversy, and while you advocate your position strongly, make sure that those on the other side know that you respect their position even though you disagree with them. If it is possible as you take a stand, show some maturity beyond your years.

One relatively easy way of gaining visibility is by writing letters to the editor. Reader surveys show that in almost all newspapers the letters to the editor have more readers than the editorials. Terry Michael heads the Washington Center for Politics and Journalism. He first became familiar to Illinois political leaders—including Paul Simon—when he wrote letters to the editor of the *St. Louis Post-Dispatch*. Those letters written as a high school student helped to launch his career, which included years as a press secretary to Paul Simon in the U.S. House and service as a press secretary to a presidential campaign.

There are four fundamental rules in writing letters to the editor:

Know what you are talking about.

Be accurate.

Be fair.

Be brief.

You may want to send a letter to the editor of your high school or college paper, or to the local newspaper, or (as a long shot) to *Time, Newsweek,* or *U.S. News and World Report.* You are not likely to have your letter printed in the magazines, but if you follow the four points just mentioned, you have a chance of having it printed and you will impress your teacher or instructor and local political leaders. It's worth a try.

B ecoming visible usually does not come from a television appearance, or a letter to the editor, or some dramatic act; but in small ways, piece by piece, you add to a mosaic so that when people see you or see your name, they automatically associate you with good things and with leadership. A letter of thanks to the best teachers you have had in grade school and high school will both startle and please those few teachers who are unaccustomed to such thoughtfulness. That sets you apart. A note of thanks to your minister for a good sermon would please him or her. Thanking a waitress for the food she brings you in a restaurant may seem like a small thing, but most people don't do it. If friends of your family are celebrating their 50th wedding anniversary, they would be pleased to receive a letter of congratulations from you, and so would their family.

Visibility also comes from doing things we spoke of earlier in this book: becoming an officer of your class or a club to which you belong or some group outside your school. If you do these things, people will think of you in leadership terms.

There also is at least one community need for which you could contribute time and leadership. Perhaps it's a shelter for the homeless; maybe you have old and neglected cemeteries that need attention; possibly there is no place in your area where battered and abused

women and children can go for safety. You are in an unusual community indeed if there are not needs. Sometimes we are so comfortable looking at our community that we fail to see the needs. Try to take a fresh look, and when you spot deficiencies, ask yourself where you and some of your friends could be effective in bringing about change. That's leadership, and your local newspaper or radio or television station probably will be interested in doing a story on your endeavors once they see concrete things happening.

Don't do something solely because it may advance your future. That is too self-serving and becomes obvious to at least some others. But if you do something because you feel it needs to be done—because you care—that also will become apparent to others. However, there is nothing morally wrong with recognizing that when you do something positive, it will help you politically. Jonathan Daniels wrote of President Calvin Coolidge, "No moral fervor moved him." People should see you acting because you are moved by concerns that are real. If they are real, that can move you into a lifetime of leadership.

Senator Jacob Javits, a distinguished Republican Senator from New York, lost his race for reelection and, shortly after his loss, he learned he had Lou Gehrig's disease, a slow disintegration of the nervous system. We could see this vigorous man gradually decline physically, though not mentally. About eight weeks before he died, someone wheeled him into Paul Simon's Senate office, hooked up a device that kept him breathing, and the former New York Senator started lobbying Paul on a measure that interested him. When Senator Javits finished talking, Paul told him, "Jack, you're an inspiration." The former Senator replied, "Paul, you have to have a mission in life." Near death, he continued to find satisfaction in helping others.

Perhaps there is a local chapter of Habitat for Humanity near you. This is a group that works to build homes and repair houses for people in need. People who turn out to help are well motivated, and they are leadership types, even though they may not consider themselves that.

If you volunteer to help, you will be broadening your contacts and making a favorable impression on men and women who could assist your political career at some time in the future.

Be creative. That's part of good leadership. Ask yourself where you could be of help to others. Inevitably that will lead to greater visibility, and that can help you launch a political career. But if you decide in 5 or 10 years that you do not want to venture into political life as a candidate, the creative things that you do to help your community will give you satisfaction in the years to come, starting a lifetime habit of service.

A good habit to have.

Personal Political Narratives

Gaining a Foothold in Queens

MARIO CUOMO

Amidst the stores and tenements of South Jamaica, in Queens in New York, where I was born and raised, there wasn't much talk or feeling about politics. In fact, there were no politics or politicians. No one ever saw a campaign sign or a campaigner. The truth was that most of the people never went to the polls, so there wasn't much point in pursuing them if all you wanted was a vote. Of course, if you were some do-gooder that wanted to help people, it would have been exactly the place to be, but there didn't seem to be any do-gooder politicians at the time, with one exception, and he wasn't from the neighborhood. His name was Franklin Roosevelt, and to the strugglers of South Jamaica, in the years of the Depression and the Second World War, he was more an icon than an individual.

So I grew into adulthood without the slightest consideration of any active involvement in politics. I went to college, played professional baseball, met Matilda and married her, went to law school, started a family, and began work as a lawyer without so much as a serious conversation about what was happening in our political world.

Looking back, I suspect the first glimmer of an interest was when I was 28 or so. As an eager, struggling young lawyer, I was retained by a group of scrap dealers and junkyard owners in Willets Point, Queens. Robert Moses was trying to take their land and their businesses so that they would not be what he regarded as an unsightly presence during the World's Fair in 1964, which was going to be built in the area. It took me three years, but we finally beat the vaunted Mr. Moses in a lawsuit that he claimed was his first major defeat. That victory attracted the attention of some homeowners in Corona,

CONTINUED

Queens, who were being threatened by Mayor Lindsay and a city administration that wanted to bulldoze an entire community of 100 homes or so to build a high school. This, it seemed to me, was another gross miscarriage of common sense and fairness by government. After six years of litigation, in 1972 we won a compromise that saved most of the homes.

The victory in Corona was a memorable experience. Many of those who lived there had never known another home. When confronted by the power of a government they did not know and believed they could not affect, they felt nothing but fear and confusion. To have dealt with that power—indeed, fought with it—and survived, exhilarated them. It gave them a new sense of assurance and comfort with a system of laws and government that until then had been mostly a tax bill, a policeman, and a summons to war. The experience had much the same effect on me.

A third struggle with government and the law followed in a place called Forest Hills. The City of New York tried to build a housing project in a middle-class community that was afraid it would destroy the neighborhood. There developed what appeared to be an irreconcilable and bitterly hostile dispute with ugly racial and religious implications. Mayor Lindsay surprised everyone by asking me to mediate the conflict. It was an unusual assignment—perhaps even a unique one. I wasn't a party to the controversy or a public official, and I wasn't even a mediator. But despite the novelty and uncertainty, I found the chance to help irresistible. After several months of discussion, negotiation, and public hearings, I was able to work out an arrangement that was reluctantly accepted by the contending groups but eventually proved to be a successful project.

The Willets Point, Corona, and Forest Hills episodes were all heavily publicized and led almost naturally to opportunities for public service. Mayor

Lindsay offered me a number of commissioner-level appointments; political leaders suggested I run for everything from Borough President to Governor, and some newspaper columnists invited me to enter the lists.

I was—understandably, I think—most reluctant to give up any part of what had become a fulfilling life. But as our personal good fortune had increased, all of us in the family had felt a growing obligation to try to give something more back to the system that had made our own lives so comfortable. And so, in 1974, I ran for office for the first time in a race for the Lieutenant Governor's position on the Democratic line. I lost.

But there were victories to follow.

Mario Cuomo, for 12 years Governor of New York, is widely remembered for his inspirational keynote address at the 1984 Democratic National Convention.

"How Do You Type?"

SANDRA DAY O'CONNOR

I grew up on a cattle ranch in rural Arizona near the New Mexico border. My grandfather had started the ranch—known as the "Lazy B" ranch—in 1870, and my father ran the ranch for his entire life. When it was time for grade school, I went away to El Paso, Texas, to live temporarily with my grandparents; the area surrounding the ranch was so sparsely populated that there were no schools nearby. But even when I went away, the "Lazy B" ranch was always "home."

After graduating high school, I left Arizona to attend Stanford University in California. While I was there, I encountered a wonderful teacher named Harry Rathburn. Professor Rathburn held seminars at his home to discuss personal ethics and goals and how each of us can make a difference in this complex world. He was brilliant; he was kind; he was inspiring; and he was a lawyer. I decided to attend law school because he demonstrated so clearly that law can be a great instrument for the social good.

In 1952, I graduated from Stanford Law School. Unfortunately, despite my good grades, no law firm in California at that time would hire a woman to be a lawyer. During an interview I was asked, "How do you type?" I answered, "Not very well," and politely informed them that my life's ambition went beyond typing. I thus gravitated toward public service and became a Deputy County Attorney for San Mateo County, California.

After some time in Europe, my husband and I moved back to Arizona in 1957, and again none of the private law firms were hiring women attorneys. I began a small law practice with one partner, and I began to serve the Phoenix, Arizona, community through a wide range of community service activities.

After having three children, I reentered public service as an Assistant Attorney General for the State of Arizona. In a few years, I was appointed state Senator. I served in the Arizona state senate for six years, where I eventually became the Majority Leader. In 1974, I entered a different branch of government—the judiciary—when I was elected as a Superior Court Judge for Maricopa County. I served as a trial judge for five years until Governor Bruce Babbitt, now Secretary of the Interior for the United States, appointed me to the Arizona Court of Appeals.

In 1981, Justice Potter Stewart retired from the Supreme Court of the United States, and President Ronald Reagan nominated me to fill the vacancy. That fall, the Senate confirmed my nomination, and I began serving as an Associate Justice. From day one, my work at the Supreme Court has been extremely interesting. The Court must consider thousands of cases each year to choose the ones that it will hear. My colleagues and I are all lawyers, and most of us have been judges on other courts, although neither is a formal requirement.

Without question, my greatest professional satisfaction has come from my opportunities in public service. The insight that I gained in college that the law can be a powerful instrument for social good inspired me to attend law school, and it has continued to inspire me throughout my career. Each of my positions in the public sector has been tremendously satisfying, from Deputy Attorney in San Mateo County to state Senator in Arizona to Associate Justice of the Supreme Court. And since my appointment to the Supreme Court in 1981, I have been honored to serve my country in this fashion. I believe that my presence on the Court signals to young people that no job is beyond their grasp. I hope that the path I have followed inspires others to pursue careers in public service.

Sandra Day O'Connor, nominated in 1981 by President Ronald Reagan, became the first woman ever appointed to be a Supreme Court Justice.

9 | **Select Your Target**

If you want to become a candidate, you cannot talk about it forever. At some point, you have to take the plunge and jump into the political waters in a daring way.

What office you first decide to run for will depend on the community in which you live and its politics. If you live in a district that is heavily Democratic or Republican, the primary will probably be your main hurdle. But frequently in those areas, a weak opposition party is desperate for candidates and may welcome you with open arms.

Paul Simon first decided to run as a candidate for the Illinois state legislature. He had just returned from two years of military service in Europe, and he already had a reputation as a tough, hard-hitting local newspaper editor. He had made a lot of regular Democrats so unhappy that, when he announced his candidacy, the executive committee of the Madison County Democratic Party voted unanimously to oppose him in the Democratic primary. He put his campaign together, worked hard, and, at the age of 25, won. A good and determined candidate can overcome opposition within his own party.

Mike Dukakis, on the other hand, decided to try his hand at municipal politics first. In Massachusetts municipal elections are, with some exceptions, nonpartisan, and in Mike's hometown, the legislative body is known as the representative town meeting, an offshoot of the old New England system of open meetings where anyone living there could show up and vote on major issues before the town. When some New England towns got too big for an open town meeting, they opted for what in effect is a town legislature of more than 200 people elected from the various precincts in town. It's not a particularly difficult office to win if you are willing to ring every doorbell in a

precinct with, at most, 3,000 voters. It is a great way to get started in politics. Only after Mike won a seat in the town meeting did he begin organizing the campaign to unseat the incumbent Democratic party organization and subsequently run successfully, as Paul had done earlier, for the state legislature.

B efore you make a decision about what office to seek, it is probably a good idea to spend some time studying the voting patterns in past elections. What do they tell you? Is there an incumbent, and, if so, is he or she vulnerable? What kind of turnout are you likely to get in the upcoming primary or final election? If the voting percentages in the district are low, or many people who voted simply skipped voting for your potential opponent, does that reflect a lack of support for the incumbent and a target of opportunity for you?

If the incumbent is not running again, that usually provides even greater possibilities.

Spend some time quietly sounding out people in the district. That doesn't mean that they know much about the politics of the place. People who are supposed to be "experts" in the politics of a particular district often have lost touch or aren't aware of the young, new voters in the district about which they are supposed to know so much.

Lloyd Bentsen, the former U.S. Senator from Texas and the first Secretary of the Treasury in the Clinton administration, who was Mike's running mate for Vice President in the 1988 presidential campaign, loves to tell the story of how he first ran for county office in south Texas after returning from the service in World War II. He dutifully visited the party bosses, who patted him on the head, told him they would make sure he wasn't disgraced in losing, and guaranteed him enough votes to make his loss respectable. Bentsen proceeded to organize young families, especially housewives, who had begun settling in the district with their returning GI husbands and owed no loyalty of any kind to the party leaders. He won, and a few years later he was on his way to the U.S. Congress.

Some self-styled experts will recommend taking a poll before you run, but polling in local elections is worthless. No one knows you anyway, so don't be surprised if you barely register in early polls. It is the kind of dogged campaigning out in the neighborhoods that so many of us have done that wins local elections, and polls can't possibly measure the impact of that kind of campaigning in the early stages of an election season.

Pollsters in local elections can't measure intensity either, and that is always a big factor in elections. How seriously committed you and your volunteers are is a big part of winning, and more than one long-shot candidate has won an election because he or she was able to mobilize people who felt strongly about the candidate and the issues.

You are going to run to win. But sometimes that isn't possible. On the other hand, a strong losing campaign may set the stage for a successful next run. Both of us have tasted defeat in the course of our political careers. Both of us were able to come back and win subsequent elections. Nobody likes to lose. But if you run a good, hard campaign and do it with dignity and real commitment, the fact that you lose is not the end of the road. It may, in fact, be the beginning.

Don't be afraid to start at the bottom, however. Each of us ran for essentially local office—Paul for a state legislative seat; Mike for a seat on a large, unpaid town legislature that meets only five or six times a year. Both of us believe that we were a lot more effective in higher office because we started at the grassroots. The late Governor Adlai Stevenson of Illinois, twice a presidential candidate, once told Paul that he wished that he had served at least one term in the state legislature before being elected Governor because he would have been a more effective Governor. That doesn't mean that occasionally someone can't vault into high office without having served an apprenticeship at the local level, but that local experience is very valuable. Usually you have to have independent financial means to start at a high office, and few of us have that kind of money. In our experience, those who begin at a low level are more effective as they move up the ladder because of the experience and understanding that those local campaigns and office-holding give us. In short, don't be afraid to start at the bottom.

O nce in office, however, you have to make your mark. That means, as we have already urged, focusing on one or two key issues, particularly if you are a member of a legislative body, and making yourself a real expert with real credibility in those policy areas. It means working hard with groups interested in these causes. It means using the media effectively, something that came easily to Paul because of his newspaper experience but now involves more than merely the local newspapers. TV, radio, videotape, the Internet—the new world of electronic communication will play a greater and greater role in American politics, and those of you who decide to run for office will have to take these new forms of media just as seriously as we took the local newspapers. But don't forget the newspapers. Although newspaper readership is declining in this country, the morning newspaper is the first thing TV assignment editors reach for—after their morning coffee—when they decide where to send their reporters for the stories that will appear on the six o'clock news. So, while fewer people may be reading the daily newspaper, what is in the front-page headlines may have a powerful influence on what others see on the nightly news. A majority of the American people get most of their information about what is going on in the world from their television sets, but leaders read the newspapers also.

Don't forget radio. And don't forget local access cable TV. It is relatively new, but a surprisingly large number of people watch it at some time during the day or week. Mike did a talk at a local senior housing complex two years ago in one of his Hawaiian shirts on the subject of universal health care. The local cable television station has run that talk dozens of times in the last two years, and he is constantly being stopped in the street by people who say, "I saw you on television last night." "In the Hawaiian shirt?" he asks. "That's the one," they reply. His talk on universal health care—a subject that Mike has mastered—is still being shown, and many are watching it. So don't take local cable lightly.

TO SUM UP: Take the plunge, and do it at a young age. We were both in our twenties when we first ran for and won public office.

REMEMBER: Without risk, there is no reward. Don't listen to your cautious friends who keep telling you to wait until the time is ripe.

THAT TIME MAY NEVER ARRIVE.

 **Personal Political Narratives**

Free Markets and Less Intervention

PHIL GRAMM

I think I must have come to public service the same way most of us do, with a common desire to make a better future for our children, but through a unique set of circumstances. How else could an obscure economics teacher be propelled into the U.S. Senate?

I recognize that the circumstances that brought me here probably will never recur, but I also understand that in America, every story of individual achievement involves unique circumstances, and there are millions of them. As those who know me have heard me say often enough, America is not a great and powerful nation because the most brilliant and talented people in the world came to live here—America is great and powerful because it is here that the most ordinary citizens are routinely afforded the opportunity to do extraordinary things. I'm living proof that the American system works.

My own story is simple enough. The son of an Army sergeant and an Alabama textile mill worker, I grew up poor. I didn't take well to schooling at first, and flunked the third, seventh, and ninth grades, but I was blessed with a mother who simply refused to accept my failures. My father died when I was 15, so she single-handedly prodded me through high school and college to a Ph.D. in economics.

In graduate school, I had set the goal of becoming a full professor by the time I was 30, and I achieved that. In the meantime, I'd met and married Dr. Wendy Lee, also an economist, and we had two children. Those were the days of America's great energy crisis, and I was increasingly concerned

about public policy, in particular about serious legislative proposals to begin rationing gasoline. I didn't know it, but for all those reasons, I'd reached the nexus of a career change in the mid-1970s. I looked at my two small boys and considered what their lives might be like in a country besieged by endless energy shortages and a growing belief that there were real limits on the future of America, and the economist-father in me concluded two things: a freer market and a little less government would cure America's most pressing problems and help both my children and my country, and I might be able to do something to make that happen.

It started with an article that *The Wall Street Journal* published which traced the fall of whale oil and the rise of the petroleum industry in the nineteenth-century economy. I believed it demonstrated that markets worked, then and now. Remember, this was a panicky time when people were lining up for hours for the privilege of buying half a tank of regular gasoline, and gas station attendants were packing pistols to fend off angry customers, so my little article got some attention.

For the first time, people I didn't know wrote to me about an important public policy. Just a handful, but it seemed that others might want to hear more about a market solution to the energy crisis, so I mailed a hundred letters to civic groups all over Texas, offering to come and speak to them. Interest was lower than I'd hoped. Exactly one reply came back, from the Lions Club of Wortham, Texas. "Thank you, Lord," I said, and drove off to Wortham. Fully a dozen Lions showed up at lunch to hear me explain my cure for the energy crisis, including a printer from down the road at Mexia, a man named Dicky Flatt.

It is fair to say that I was not a hit on the speaking circuit, but I made some friends and ultimately, offers began to trickle in. In time, the Senate Energy

CONTINUED

Committee invited me to testify. I came, I testified, I went home. When I got back to College Station, Texas, Wendy asked me how it went. I told her that I thought I could explain what I had seen in Washington with a story. It was, I said, as though a great sheet of paper had blown into the city and affixed itself to the top of the Capitol dome, blotting out the sun. Below, lawmakers thought if the sky went dark in Washington, the entire world must be in the dark. They were groping for solutions. The Democrats had plenty of ideas, but they seemed to coalesce around a plan to build an artificial sun for $100 million. Now, the Republicans back then hadn't had an idea in years, but they were absolutely opposed to the Democrats' idea. Yet they were willing to compromise: the sun would be built for $50 million, it would be constructed by private contractors and the government would regulate it. I told her that nobody in Washington had figured out that they just needed to rip the paper off the Capitol.

It was about then that I decided to run for public office. Now, I might have run for a House seat or tried to get an appointive policy job, but I was thinking much bigger than that, so I ran against U.S. Senator Lloyd Bentsen. In the end, it was like an armadillo had challenged a Mack Truck. I lost, big.

After Wendy scraped me off the pavement, I begged her to forgive me for throwing away our life's savings. She not only forgave me, but when I began to think about trying one last time, she agreed. Two years later I ran for the seat being vacated by retiring U.S. Representative Olin "Tiger" Teague, and won.

In a district that stretched hundreds of miles from the outskirts of Dallas and Fort Worth to the suburbs of Houston, I asked people to send me to Washington to do what they would do themselves. I told them that I would work to balance the budget and to get the government off their backs and

out of their pockets. In essence, I said that if they'd boost me up, I'd try to tear the paper off the Capitol dome. I've never stopped trying.

Phil Gramm, a senior Senator from Texas in the 106th Congress, had first served as a Democrat in the House of Representatives. He resigned his position and then successfully ran as a Republican for a seat in the U.S. Senate. In 1996, he also ran for the Republican nomination for President.

Announce and Then File Your Petitions

No, you're probably not ready to announce your candidacy tomorrow or next year. But Paul Simon once had a student in his class at Southern Illinois University, William Bodine, who became a Republican candidate for township trustee at the age of 18—and got elected! He will be running for higher office in the future.

First, you have to decide what office you want to pursue. By starting at a lower level, Bill Bodine increased his chances of being elected, and he learned the process in a practical way. He circulated petitions in his rural area, getting as many people as he could to sign. Why? If someone signs your petition, he or she feels a semi-obligation to vote for you in an election. Then Bill took campaigning seriously, and the result startled—and pleased—many people that someone not through college had shown an interest in government and in getting elected. Residents in the area knew his parents as hard-working farmers, respected them, and had a sense that "young Bill" had the same attributes.

Ira Jackson was elected to the Brookline, Massachusetts, town meeting when he was 18. He subsequently became Associate Dean of the John F. Kennedy School of Government at Harvard and Mike Dukakis's state revenue commissioner.

If you run for a township office or for the city council of a small city, calling a press conference to announce your candidacy does not

make sense. But preparing a five- or six-paragraph story that you take to the newspapers, radio, and television stations is worthwhile. But don't expect great coverage! If you're fortunate, one of them may do a feature story on you. More likely, your five-paragraph story will be condensed into one or two paragraphs. But it is a start.

If you have a friend who is a reporter, or even know a reporter slightly, take a rough draft of your announcement to that person and ask for advice. Probably he or she will give it to you, but in any event the reporter will know you a little better, and all of us are pleased when someone comes asking for our suggestions. Having an above-average ego is true of most people in politics and journalism. There is a level of self-confidence a person has who believes that he or she can contribute either as a public official or by writing about public affairs. You have to believe in yourself.

Make your media announcement brief. If you have five paragraphs, one paragraph will be for the office you seek, two paragraphs can be on the issues you intend to stress, and the other two part of your biography—that part of your experience that might incline people to consider your candidacy.

If you can get a respected public or party official to endorse your candidacy at the time of the announcement, that is worth doing. Endorsements generally do not translate directly into votes, but the right type of endorsement can cause voters to seriously consider voting for you.

If you seek a state legislative position or perhaps even a race for the U.S. House, then it is worth having a formal press conference at which you should make a brief statement. We stress brevity because the longer your statement, the less control you have over what is used by the media. If you have a punchy two-point program and you stress that in your press release and in your statement, it is likely to be picked up by the newspapers as well as TV and radio. Use simple, plain language. Don't try to impress people with technical jargon. The great speeches of history used language everyone could understand.

If in your prepared statement you have words you would not use in your ordinary conversation, drop those words.

After your brief statement at a press conference, you should open it up for questions from reporters—and don't be too disappointed if only one or two journalists show up. You'll experience some of that the rest of your political career. Before that announcement and those questions, however, try to get on top of issues as much as possible. Have two or three of your sharpest friends listen to your mock announcement followed by their questions. Have them be tough on you, and refine the answers so that you show you are knowledgeable, but that you can be brief. A "great" five-minute answer is not going to make radio or television. If you make television, it is not likely to be for more than 10 or 20 seconds, but those 10 or 20 seconds can be extremely helpful to you. What 10-second sound bite can you give them? Practice it.

If you run for the state legislature or Congress, have a small group of people there—or a larger group if you can—to generate enthusiasm and to give reporters or television cameras the appearance of a campaign that is alive and vibrant. If you have a theme, have a canvas sign in back of you, with its few words. That might make a newspaper photo or a television camera shot. (Don't use the theme that Governor Edwin Edwards of Louisiana used after serving as Governor and then leaving the office facing legal difficulties. He then ran again. His theme: "Bring the Rascals Back!" Amazingly, he won.)

Plan early for the few days after your announcement so that you create the atmosphere of momentum. It is also a good time to take advantage of whatever publicity your announcement has received—probably not enough to please you. If your statement of candidacy made television, that is a powerful plus. People ordinarily respond to television as to no other medium. Even children come up and ask, "Aren't you on television?" It creates immediate semi-celebrity status.

Frequently the announcement coincides with your signing or circulating your petitions. If you run for city office, the city clerk can give you the blank petition forms and advise you when to file them. The county clerk does the same for county office, and for statewide office either the Secretary of State or your state's election board usually is the source of that information.

Read the forms carefully and make sure you fill in all the required information accurately. Have someone you trust look it over closely. If your forms are not properly filled out, your opponent might be able to have you removed from the ballot. A few states also require that you sign an oath of loyalty to the United States.

If running for the city council requires 50 signatures from registered voters, get 100 to sign. Almost certainly a few of the signatures you get will be invalid. People forget that they are no longer registered, or they are too embarrassed to admit they are not registered so they sign, and sometimes in a gesture of good will a man will sign his wife's name or a wife will sign her husband's name, and those not signed by the person are invalid.

Make a copy of your petitions for your protection. If questions arise about the validity of some of the signatures, you can answer the questions. Equally important, once you file for office, send a letter to those who signed your petitions thanking them for helping to launch your career. Some names will be almost unreadable. Don't send a letter to someone misspelling that person's name. Check the name in a telephone book or in some other way, and if you are not certain of the spelling, don't send the letter.

And be prepared for the most important question that will be asked you by friends, reporters, and curious citizens: Why are you running for office? It is amazing how frequently candidates are not prepared with a good answer to that question.

"Well begun is half done," the poet Horace wrote more than 2,000 years ago. There is some truth to that observation. Make sure that applies to your campaign.

Personal Political Narratives

Once I Gained Confidence

SUSAN MOLINARI

My father was a member of Congress. His father was a member of the New York state assembly. Running for public office may have been presumed for me by others, but it certainly was no certainty as far as I was concerned.

Needless to say, I was raised to believe that public service was an honorable profession and one that would bring great gratification and intrinsic rewards. I felt comfortable in the arena, as our living room was the site of many fundraisers and our kitchen table the spot for many campaign plans.

For many years I was comfortable in playing in the background, organizing rallies, helping to write speeches. It never occurred to me that one day I would be the candidate. It never occurred to me that one day I would *want* to be the candidate. Then one day when I was approached to run for the New York assembly, I had to face the fact that I was just plain scared.

I was afraid of the challenge—afraid of the possibility of failure. I was really afraid of embarrassing my parents and hurting my dad's reputation. Once I recognized that it was my own confidence that was holding me back from tremendous and exciting opportunities, I had to do it. By then it was too late to run for the assembly, but a seat was soon to open up on the New York City Council.

It wasn't too long before I got rid of my sea legs and I knew the issues. I even had some answers, good answers. My first race for the council was decided after a 10-day recount by 161 votes. And let me tell you, I worked hard for those votes. I went to the train stations in the morning, shopping

centers in the afternoon, the train, bus, and ferry stations in the evenings, ending the day going door-to-door.

As exhausting as every campaign is, I wouldn't have missed one. I have met my closest friends during campaigns. Smart, loyal people who believed in my philosophy, liked my analysis of problems, thought it was cool that I was so young (26 when I first announced for office), great that I was a woman—whatever the reason, they made it a team effort. It became a lot less about me and more about the cause.

I have since run six more times, for re-election to the city council and then to succeed my father in Congress. I have championed ideas and causes that will live with me forever. I have fought against domestic violence and child abuse, worked on legislation involving our nation's railroads, and fought for issues surrounding national defense, and was a member of the budget committee that produced the first balanced budget in a generation. My last bill on one of my last days in Congress was to authorize the post office to produce a stamp above cost with the proceeds to go toward finding a cure for breast cancer. My grandmother died of breast cancer, and I am hopeful that my daughter, her namesake, will be secure in her adult life in knowing that there is a cure. I had a job that allowed me to be a part of every woman's dream. Surely that was worth facing my insecurities and taking a gamble that I could fail. Clearly I wouldn't do it any other way.

When I first approached my father and told him that I wanted to run for office but I was afraid of the critics, the worst one being myself, he gave me a quote by Theodore Roosevelt to read. It continues to inspire me and fortify me when the going gets a little tough:

> "The credit belongs to the man who is actually in the arena. Whose
> face is marred by dust and sweat and blood. Who strives valiantly,

CONTINUED

Once I Gained Confidence CONTINUED

who errs and comes short again and again, who knows the great
enthusiasms, the great devotions, who spends himself in a worthy
cause. Who, at the best, knows in the end the triumph of high achievement, and who at the worst, at least fails while daring greatly, so that
his place shall never be with those timid souls who know neither
victory nor defeat."

*Susan Molinari, a former Republican Congresswoman from New York, was
elected in 1990 and reelected for four terms in Congress. She is widely
remembered for her inspirational keynote speech at the 1996 Republican
convention.*

| **Personal Political Narratives**

My Neighbors Asked Me to Run

CAROL MOSELEY-BRAUN

Some people know what they want to do with their lives from an early age. I was not one of them. In fact, I have continually been mystified how I wound up doing a particular thing at a particular time in my life. It seemed so much to depend on serendipity (which is another way to say unexpected good fortune).

I grew up in a home in which both parents worked. I remember my father as being primarily in law enforcement, but over time he "moonlighted," or worked part time, in occupations ranging from musician to insurance salesman. My mother was a medical technician, a relatively new field at the time she entered it, and especially unusual for an African American. Of course, in those days they called themselves Negroes.

My father was probably the most influential in directing my career choices. He enjoyed philosophy and was always concerned about the world around him. I learned about religions because he took me to various churches, synagogues, and temples. I learned about unions because he took me to rallies and meetings of the Packinghouse Workers. I learned about segregation when our family integrated a Chicago neighborhood.

My mother was the rock of stability in our family. She was much more focused on family issues, and protected us—sometimes even from our father—in keeping with her steady, conservative style. She was a great one for "sayings," expressions of the wisdom of the "old folks." She emphasized hard work, and diligence, and the pursuit of excellence. She instilled in us the notion that your work product is a reflection of who you are, and will

CONTINUED

stand as a representation of your effort and ability. She would tell us: "When a job is once begun, never stop until it's done. Be the task large or small, do it right or not at all." Of course, on more than one occasion we volunteered not to do it at all.

I was the oldest of four children. This might not be all that relevant, but in my mind it was an important reason why I did not become a scholar or academic. I was always called upon to take care of the others, and took my first job at the age of 15 in order to supplement our mother's income: she and my dad divorced at that time, and she was very hard pressed to support us by herself. So school, frankly, had to take a back seat to my duty to my family, whether it was in holding a part-time job or keeping the house. I was always "responsible," even when I resented it.

There was never any question but that I would go to college. Both my parents had attended college, and it was simply assumed that I would prepare for a professional career. Midway through my first year at the University of Illinois, however, I got another idea, and dropped out.

This was one of my first introductions to serendipity. Sometimes, things that seem good turn out to be terrible, and things that seem misfortune turn out to be good. That is what happened to me when I dropped out of school.

I got a really high-paying, interesting dream job working for the Chicago Housing Authority (CHA). But the riots broke out, and my immediate supervisor sent me out to go door-to-door to ask the residents not to participate in the riot. Then she went home. I will never forget wearing a yellow hard hat with CHA stamped on the front of it, hunkered down next to a smokestack, waiting for my next chance to dash between buildings without getting shot while the pop pop pop sound of gunshot rang in my ears. What really infuriated

me, though, was not the rioting residents, but the middle management, who fled to their cars at the first sign of trouble. Pressed up against a wall, in a flash of inspiration, I decided to go back to school.

I went back to the University of Illinois, this time at the Chicago campus, and put aside the "pre-med" major my mother had urged me to take, and went into political science instead. My time at CHA had raised questions in my mind about our social order, and about poverty, segregation, and the status of women. I wanted to understand better that which I had simply reacted to, and to have some foundation for the opinions I had formed in spite of my lack of education. College broadened my mind and my horizons, and left me excited about learning. As much to the point, it expanded my life options and gave me opportunity to engage in a lot more careers than would have been available to me with just a high school education.

A second bit of serendipity came as I was about to graduate from college. It was a time of real political activism, with campus activity against the war in Vietnam, the Black Power movement, the more conservative civil rights movement, women's liberation, and a blossoming environmental movement. (I ran for, and became, secretary of our student government on the "Action" party slate, my first elected office.) Over a game of cards with some college friends, I came across an application to take the Law School Admissions Test. Law school! My father had briefly gone to law school, and it seemed then like a sensible alternative to the fog I was in about my career. I signed up to take the LSAT.

The University of Chicago was the only law school to which I made application. In hindsight, if the Dean there hadn't accepted me, I would probably never have become a lawyer, or had such an impressive credential, or had many of the opportunities it made possible.

CONTINUED

At this point it is important to note that it had never occurred to me that a black woman from a working-class background could not become a lawyer. In fact, one of the secrets of my success has been personal oblivion to limitations of my race or gender or class or physical capacity. This may sound like a good thing, but in fact it has caused as many problems as it has created opportunities. I probably should have paid more careful attention to the realities of racism and sexism. That I did not do so has been both a blessing and a curse.

I was one of eight blacks and about a dozen women in my class at the law school. A professor, Soia Mentschikoff, became something of a role model for my legal ambitions, and a guest lecturer, State Senator Richard Newhouse, introduced me to electoral politics. In those days, the civil rights movement was separate from elected politics, but Senator Newhouse argued that they had to come together on behalf of the public interest. Professor Mentschikoff maintained that one had to first understand the law before attempting to change it. With different approaches, they taught me to think in terms of what can be, and then to work toward it through political action.

All of this is, of course, prologue to my last 20 years in elected office. Following law school, I became an Assistant United States Attorney and spent four years representing the people of the United States in court. I left that office to start a family, but shortly after my son Matthew was born, a group of neighbors approached me to stand for election to the state legislature. I had gotten involved with a local environmental issue, and without knowing it, those activities brought me to the attention of the political activists in the community. Once again serendipity played a role, although I am not certain that it was not a challenge that made me take up the suggestion to run for office. Some people who had another candidate in mind told me that I could not possibly win because the blacks wouldn't vote for me

because I was not part of the Chicago machine, the whites wouldn't vote for me because I was black, and nobody would vote for me because I was a woman. It was a dare I couldn't refuse. After a tough door-to-door effort, I won election as state Representative.

That was the beginning of my career in electoral politics. I became an Assistant Majority Leader in the state legislature, an executive officer in Cook County as Recorder of Deeds, and later a United States Senator. In each of these offices, I have tried to make a difference for good, and to make our system of government one that responds to the needs of all of the people. My public service was made possible, however, by three things: good fortune, hard work, and belief that God wants us all to use the talents we are given to be the most that we can be.

Carol Moseley-Braun made history in 1992 by becoming the first African-American woman ever elected to the United States Senate. She served one term before going on to become Ambassador to New Zealand.

| # The Campaign

Nothing is more exciting—or more intense—than a political campaign at any level. There are a thousand things to do and never enough time to do them well. Organizing, fundraising, door-to-door canvassing, making speeches, debating the issues, getting out the vote on Election Day, and waiting for the returns on election night—these are all part of what makes politics fascinating and worthwhile.

What office you run for will have much to do with the kind of campaign that you run. If it is something as low on the totem pole as a seat in the Brookline, Massachusetts, town meeting for which Mike Dukakis first ran, it is basic politics. His district had approximately 3,000 voters, but only one polling place. He had to print 3,000 hand-out cards; get himself a comfortable pair of walking shoes; and knock on about 1,500 doors (assuming an average of two voters per doorbell). He did this mostly on weekends, and he also spent a full 13 hours in front of the polling place in his precinct on Election Day. Getting his constituents to give him one of their seven votes wasn't that difficult, and they did so.

For Paul Simon, however, who decided to run for the legislature from a district with a population of 160,000, that first try was tougher. He also ran against two Democratic incumbents, and he had virtually no support among the party regulars. What do you do under those circumstances? You file your petitions, put a campaign organization together, get as many volunteers as you can, work your head off, and, if you do it well, you win, and Paul won decisively.

At whatever level you run, however, there are certain basic building blocks that must be part of every campaign. One, as we have strongly suggested earlier in this book, has to be a first-rate grassroots

organization. Break down your district into working pieces. Sometimes the existing voting precincts themselves are a natural framework. In Mike's legislative campaigns, he ran from a district with about 60,000 voters and 12 voting precincts. The core of his campaign organization was always his 12 precinct captains. They, in turn, were responsible for recruiting 25 or 30 precinct workers, each of whom was assigned responsibilities within the precinct—everything from canvassing to phone banking to getting bumper stickers on people's cars (with their approval, of course) and sending out 25 or 50 "Dear Friend" cards to people they knew in the legislative district.

Paul did something very similar, relying heavily on student volunteers.

Where did Mike and Paul find their precinct leaders? They recruited them, mostly from the district, and the key people were all volunteers. But they believed in their candidates; they worked hard; and some of them, too, eventually ended up running for and winning public office themselves. Without them we couldn't possibly have won. Of course, there is no substitute for the candidate's personal campaigning. Some candidates hate door-to-door canvassing in a neighborhood or in a business district. We thoroughly enjoyed it. It takes commitment to go out day after day and night after night, seven days a week for months on end. But you meet fascinating people; you get solid ideas; you learn a lot more about your district than you ever thought possible; and personal campaigning is by far the most effective way to meet people and win votes. That is particularly true these days when fewer and fewer candidates seem to want to do it. If you understand how effective it can be and are willing to put in the time and effort, most people you meet on their doorsteps will be genuinely interested and pleased to meet you, and—depending on the impression you make—will seriously consider voting for you.

inging doorbells in a residential area during working hours is probably a waste of time because these days almost everyone seems to be working. But there are other things you can do during this time period. We've already pointed out that transit and bus stops from seven to nine in the morning are naturals. Mike had 23 transit stops in his district, and he hit them all twice, once before the primary and again before the final. Rural areas, such as Paul's, are different, and an effective way to campaign is to go in and out of small-town stores, meeting clerks, customers, and everyone you can, asking their names and giving them a campaign folder. Only rarely will a store manager object. On a good day, you can meet about a thousand people in this way, many more than in going door-to-door in residential areas, although Paul did much of that, too. Supermarkets are always fair game, and while the traffic is slower during the day, at all hours there are people shopping at the local supermarket, and many will come from your district. Most people don't travel many miles to do grocery shopping.

Ethnic picnics, street and block parties, festivals and celebrations—all these, too, are naturals for you and your volunteers. We figured that when our constituents began telling us that this was the third or fourth time they had shaken our hand, we were beginning to penetrate.

While a strong and well-organized grassroots effort is, in our opinion, the absolute centerpiece of a local campaign, there are dozens of other things that must be done. You need a media strategy and someone with enough experience in press or public relations work to give you a hand. See if you can recruit a volunteer with that kind of experience. You'd be surprised at the number of people in your district who may not want to knock on doors but who have a background in press or public relations and are willing to put in long hours for you as volunteers. Paul, of course, had a big advantage because he was in the newspaper business and understood it well. Mike's communications person was the head of public relations for a large nonprofit organization who had had substantial press experience in his youth.

How much money you spend on campaign advertising is something that you and your press person will have to discuss and decide. We are not great fans of big advertising budgets for essentially local campaigns.

130

Often you are paying for a media market that extends far beyond your immediate district, and that means big money. Commercial television for a small local race is absolutely prohibitive. Cable TV is more affordable, but don't waste your money if you aren't convinced that enough people watch it to make the spending of money on ads worthwhile.

Our preference is for a limited number of well-placed ads in the local newspapers, and, in rural areas, radio commercials. Save the rest of your money for bumper stickers, mailings, and literature with which to arm yourself and your canvassers when you hit the streets. That's where you can really connect with the voters.

A nd then, there is the issue of money. How much do you need? How do you raise it? Here again, we may be in the minority, but we think the best way to raise the funds you need for local races is at the grassroots level from as broad a base of people as you can possibly find. When we first started, each of us spent a total of a little more than $3,000 in our legislative campaigns. Obviously, inflation alone requires you to raise more than that today. But we raised our money almost exclusively from small donors. Neither of us had a contribution of more than $100. We began the fundraising effort with a mailing to anyone who we thought would be willing to support us in whatever way they could. It included a return envelope and a sign-up card that asked them for a public endorsement and a variety of ways in which they could help. It also included a request for a contribution. Many people wrote a check for $10, $20, or even $50 in response to that letter.

We would invariably ask our precinct captains to organize at least one fundraising coffee party or backyard barbecue in their precinct. We'd be there and spend time meeting, greeting, and listening and talking to the guests. Our wives, Kitty and Jeanne, would often be with us. We'd make a short talk and leave plenty of time for questions. By the time the event was finished, virtually everybody there had a sense that they knew us and, hopefully, liked us. And we made sure to shake the hand of literally everyone present.

We not only were able to raise funds there; many of these people would then go out and work hard for us or at least talk favorably to their friends. So fundraising at coffees and barbecues isn't just an end in itself. It is a great way to raise the money you need and recruit volunteers.

There will be speeches to make and debates to prepare for, and successful politicians usually get to be good talkers. That doesn't mean that either one of us had gifts as spellbinding speakers when we started. And we're not sure anyone would call us that today. What we did do, especially with groups of 25 or 50 people, was convey the depth of our feelings and beliefs in a way that persuaded people to vote for us again and again; and we gradually got better at speaking in public.

Both of us tried to keep our legislative campaigns positive and not attack our opponents. That is less possible as you seek higher and higher office, particularly in these days of almost knee-jerk negative campaigning. But we are positive people, and, like most Americans, abhor the kind of mean and often unfair attack campaigning that has been a part of American politics since the beginning of the Republic. We both found, at least at the local level, that the best strategy was to be positive, stay positive, and try hard not to respond in kind to unwarranted attacks. For the most part, at the local level that approach served us well.

Election Day activities are also important. If you have organized your district and organized it well, you should have an army of people ready to work for you on Election Day. Every polling place should be covered by one of your workers—all day. If possible, your voting lists should have a telephone number next to the name of every voting household. Where it is permitted, you should have a checker inside the polling place who is legally entitled to stand or sit next to the election officials and record the people who are voting as they come in.

At about three in the afternoon, your get-out-the-vote operation does a key job. Precinct leaders pick up the voting lists from the checker with the names of those who still haven't voted. The phone banks swing into action. Each registered voter who has indicated in

your canvass that he or she either definitely will or is inclined to vote for you must get a call, or two or three calls if they still aren't home when your phone banks go to work. If possible, you should have cars available to pick them up at their homes and take them to the polls. A sizable number of people get home from work too tired to contemplate voting or going to the polls. Because someone called and offered them a ride, especially if they had met the candidate and his or her volunteers during the previous weeks, they are likely to accept and vote. Thousands of campaigns have been won or lost as the result of a first-rate get-out-the-vote effort on Election Day.

So far, we have been focusing on what are essentially local or state legislative campaigns. How does campaigning change when you decide you want to run for Congress or the United States Senate or Governor, or ultimately, the presidency of the United States?

We've tried them all, and we can tell you that the fundamentals are still the same. Intensive grassroots organization; lots of volunteers; a solid, well-conceived message that focuses on a limited number of important issues; the effective use of the media; reasonable but not extravagant advertising budgets; energy; and commitment. However, going from a legislative or local office in a district of anywhere from 3,000 to 100,000 voters, to a statewide office in Illinois with a population of 12 million, or Massachusetts with a population of 6 million requires other things as well.

You may, for example, be able to be your own campaign manager in a local or legislative race. We were. That is impossible when you are running statewide. You probably don't need to spend much money on paid media in a local race. Going statewide requires a large and effective budget for radio, TV, and the print media. You will spend more time visiting the editorial boards of your state's newspapers and dropping in on every radio station you can find to do a live interview that will be carried over and over again on drive time news.

You'll be doing some personal campaigning at factory gates and ethnic picnics, but you must build a first-rate, volunteer, grassroots organization across the state that will be knocking on doors for you. Your day will be filled with media, political appearances, policy events, and fundraising. You won't be spending anywhere near as much time in neighborhoods as when you sought local office. But if you know what you are doing, you won't neglect the grassroots that got you there in the first place. Organizational meetings, "low dollar" fund raisers, and regular appearances in the business districts or schools or recreational areas or senior centers of your state's communities will become part of your life. You will be meeting, speaking, advocating, "pressing the flesh," and making sure that the people of that particular town or county know that you were in their territory and that you care about them.

"Going statewide" is unquestionably different from campaigning at the local level. However, in some ways it is not as satisfying. The higher you go, the less contact you are likely to have with average citizens, and both of us worked hard to try to never lose that connection. That meant lots of intensive grassroots campaigning and regular town meetings and other opportunities to connect with people once we had been elected. Any officeholder who allows himself or herself to be walled off from the public is a candidate for losing the next election.

How you stay connected if you decide to run for the most important political office in the world, President of the United States, is a totally different challenge, and despite our best efforts, we're not sure either one of us has figured that out. Running for the presidency is the toughest and most intensive campaign of all, and it is simply impossible to maintain the kind of special relationship and grassroots contact that we always enjoyed with our fellow citizens as local and statewide officeholders. At first, of course, in the Iowa caucuses and small towns of New Hampshire, you can go out and campaign in the way we always did it. In fact, if you don't spend a lot of personal time with people in their homes and communities in those two states, you won't be around for the other primaries. They expect it, and it isn't difficult to do if you have had the experience we had before making the race for the presidency.

Mike spent 85 days campaigning in the state of Iowa and was personally in every one of the state's 99 counties. Paul spent a little less time there but also visited every county.

Then, however, state primaries come with a rush, and it is impossible to do more than a few days in each state as the campaign unfolds. The media play a greater and greater role, and more and more campaigning focuses on making sure that the candidate is on the local six o'clock news. The numbers of national reporters who begin covering the campaign grows dramatically. By the time we both got to New Hampshire, neither one of us could walk down a main street and do the kind of hand-shaking we loved to do in our statewide campaigns. There were as many as 30 or 40 television cameras in front of us blocking all but the most intrepid of voters who still wanted to take a look at us or grab our hands.

When in desperation you finally decide to accept Secret Service protection, the walling off from the public is more complete, and from that moment on the easy, informal relationship that we always had with the people we were trying to represent is almost impossible. The national media takes over, and if you are the nominee of your party, as Mike was, virtually all of your campaign day is spent making speeches to what you hope are large and enthusiastic crowds that will look good on the six o'clock news. If the person you are running against decides to go on the attack with a barrage of 30-second commercials accusing you of being "soft on crime" or insufficiently patriotic, you need a well-thought-out strategy for responding quickly. Otherwise, as Mike found out much to his dismay, you are going to be making a concession speech on election night.

We don't want to discourage any of you from thinking big politically—and that includes the possibility of running for the highest office in the land. But if you are seriously thinking about it, see us first. We can at least tell you what not to do, and perhaps give you some guidance about how you mount a winning campaign in the supercharged atmosphere of the presidential race.

Most of you won't run for the presidency. But you can begin now to think about running or working in local campaigns where you can have a real impact and learn a great deal at the same time.

You won't regret it.

How I Got Started in Politics

OLYMPIA J. SNOWE

I often tell graduating high school seniors that, sitting at my own graduation, it never occurred to me to think that I'd ever be a United States Senator. It never occurred to me that the daughter of a Greek immigrant would one day speak from the floor of the same United States Senate that once echoed with the words of John F. Kennedy, Henry Clay, and Daniel Webster.

I did, however, realize that I wanted to be involved in some form of public service. The form that service would take was quite another mystery, but looking back on my life, I can see that the seeds of my interest were planted early.

My parents, hard-working people—my father, an immigrant from Greece, my mother, a first-generation American—had died before I was 10, and my aunt and uncle took me into their family, which already included five children. My uncle was a barber, and my aunt worked in a textile mill—and after my uncle died, my aunt had to support me as well as her own children.

Out of those early experiences in my life grew a conviction: that no pursuit is as valuable or worthier than the simple idea of helping others—of enabling individuals to improve their lives, of softening the hardest days and brightening the darkest. For me, public service was an opportunity to act on those convictions.

My political inclinations probably first blossomed back when I was 13 years old, when I volunteered to rally votes in my school for Richard Nixon, who at the time was running for President against John F. Kennedy. We were having a mock election and, unlike out in the real world, Nixon won! While in junior high school, I also conducted my own campaign for high elective office—that is, president of the student body. I posted signs everywhere—in the hallways,

along the stone walls around the school—and I even had to make a speech in front of all my classmates. That was my first successful campaign!

Those childhood forays into the political realm not only made an impression on me, but obviously had a lasting impact. Later, at the University of Maine, I majored in political science and whetted my appetite further by spending two summers working in state government—including one in the Office of the Governor. A few years after graduating, I was elected by the local Republican City Committee to be a member of the Board of Voter Registration, and I also went to work at the district office of then-Congressman Bill Cohen (R-Maine).

During this span of time, I was privileged to work on a number of campaigns, and I always encourage young people to do the same. Volunteering to help the candidate of your choice can not only be rewarding, it can be a lot of fun and give you an opportunity to meet and talk with leaders with whom you may not otherwise have the chance to interact.

In 1973, at the age of 26, I won a special election called to fill the seat in the Maine House of Representatives held by my late husband, who had died on the way back from a legislative session. There I served until 1976, when I was elected to the Maine Senate for one term. It was at the State House that I worked for the first time with my future husband, Jock McKernan—then the Assistant House Republican Leader, later a member of Congress and Governor of Maine—and we married in 1989.

In 1978, I decided to run for Congress, and like my predecessor, Bill Cohen, I walked the Second Congressional District of Maine talking to people about their concerns and hopes for the future. That year, I was elected for the first time to the U.S. House of Representatives, where I went on to serve a total of eight terms before my election to the U.S. Senate in 1994. I felt then, as I do now, that public service is a high calling, and I've been honored to serve the people of Maine and the United States ever since.

CONTINUED

Looking back, I never could have realized that the meaning of some of my life's experiences wouldn't really surface for some years to come; that, for example, having only made it through the University of Maine with the use of student loans would teach me their critical value years later in Congress, where I led the fight to restore $10 billion in cuts to student loan programs. Or that working one summer in a Christmas-ornament factory would teach me the enormous importance of workplace safety—again, something that would surface as a significant issue in Congress. Or that, as a work-study student in state government, my exposure to a professor's emotional reaction to Soviet tanks rolling through Czechoslovakia during the Prague Spring of 1968 would eventually enrich my appreciation for that country's liberation in 1989.

So, too, did my experience in Maine's capital, Augusta, provide me with a model for good government. There, I found that politics and public life were positive and constructive endeavors. Once our elections were over, my legislative colleagues and I put campaigns and party labels behind us to enact laws that genuinely improved the lives of the citizens of our state. As leaders, I believe we must be willing to work together across the sometimes clear and sometimes vague political party lines that separate us. We must come together for the common good to meet our country's challenges, and we must never lose sight of the two enduring elements—indeed, two testaments—to our remarkable resolve as a people: a notion of the public good combined with the leadership to attain that good.

Those are the guiding principles I have tried to follow throughout my tenure in public service. For example, when I came to Congress in 1979 as one of only 17 women in both the House and Senate, I was not only determined to "go to bat" for the women of America, but I recognized that I had a tremendous responsibility and obligation to do so.

That's why, as co-chair of the Congressional Caucus for Women's Issues for a decade, I helped lead the charge to rewrite laws that worked against women and their changing roles in society—both at home and in the work-place. Together, we changed child-support laws to make "deadbeat parents" responsible. We worked to make child care more accessible, acceptable, and affordable. We changed pension laws so that a husband could no longer cancel his wife's right to his pension at whim and without notice.

And, along with two colleagues, I discovered that—incredibly, and as recently as 1999—women were being systematically excluded from clinical medical trials, like the now-infamous study trial of aspirin's ability to prevent heart attacks that included 20,000 doctors—all of them men.

These were trials with the potential to yield life-saving treatments, trials con-ducted by the National Institutes of Health—the premier research facility in the country, if not the world—and paid for by the federal government. But we changed all that, too—we mandated the inclusion of women, and legisla-tion I introduced established an Office of Women's Health Research as well at the National Institutes of Health.

Public service is a noble calling that can make a real difference in the lives of others. I hope I have lived up to the tremendous trust placed in me by the people of Maine, and I would encourage anyone who hears the call of public service to get involved and begin your own journey into this interesting and deeply rewarding field of endeavor.

Olympia J. Snowe, a Republican from Maine who served for many years as a Congresswoman, was in 1994 the first Greek-American woman elected to the United States Senate.

Law of Unintended Circumstances

PATRICIA SCHROEDER

As a student in high school and at the University of Minnesota I waded right into debates on all the bubbling issues of the day. I was always part of student government, fighting for a range of issues like better cafeteria food, moving the country on civil rights, or getting the university to stop investing in companies with ties to racist South Africa. As you can see, my student citizenship agenda was very broad-based! To me, participating in all these debates was a great privilege. If I had been born in many countries or in an earlier century than this one, legal authorities would have shut me down and who knows what else. Minnesota was one of the first universities to change their investment portfolio so there were no companies with South African ties. Every time I saw Nelson Mandela on television I felt proud of the small part I played in that country's evolution. The same pride swells up when I see progress in civil rights, women's rights, the disabled and mentally ill getting more rights, children getting better care, and the environment getting more respect. Working to make sure the next generation inherits the country in better shape than they got it is every citizen's duty. One of the best places to do that work is in the political arena.

After finishing Harvard Law School, my husband, Jim, and I decided we wanted to live in Denver, Colorado. After becoming residents, I volunteered to be legal counsel to the Rocky Mountain Planned Parenthood and the Denver Fair Housing Commission. After work, we both volunteered our legal services in legal clinics in public housing projects, worked to desegregate the public school system, participated in a book group and groups questioning the war in Vietnam, political groups, and our church. Obviously, I was

involved with many women's organizations, but even though I was very involved in public issues, I never ever thought of myself as a political candidate. Yes, I was always in the arena, but I wanted to be in the seats yelling cheers or boos rather that on the playing field taking direct hits.

My husband and I had our second baby, Jamie, in 1970. The same year Jim ran for the state legislature, losing by just a few votes. Every 10 years the Federal government takes a census. Because Americans move a lot, states redraw political districts after the census so each political district has about the same population. The Colorado legislature redrew our old district so Jim was in a new one! They didn't want him running again in 1972 and winning! But the Law of Unintended Consequences struck again. Jim didn't run in 1972, but I did. I ran for Congress instead of the state legislature. How did that happen? A mother of a six- and a two-year-old did not run for office in 1972. The professional politicians in Colorado were chortling. What kind of a kamikaze run was this woman making? To their surprise and mine, I turned out to be a winner instead of a kamikaze and have served in Congress for 24 years. I probably would not have run if I thought I could win.

Why was I crazy enough to climb down out of the "safe seats" of the public arena and expose myself to the travails of political life? When my daughter Jamie was born, I was 30 years old, and I almost died. That gets your attention! I decided to sample anything I thought might be interesting because life is fragile. Further, I was convinced by everyone who knew a lot about politics I could never win, so it appeared to be a short-term adventure ending on Election Day. Running appeared to be risk-free. I'd always approached politics safely ensconced in a classroom or in a citizens' group. Now the bright lights were on me, and I had to publicly defend my beliefs. This was a new exciting challenge, and on the first Tuesday in November it would be over. I could return to my more sheltered positions I'd occupied before.

CONTINUED

Law of Unintended Circumstances CONTINUED

Obviously, I won and never returned to the lower profile. My point is we should always use the opportunity to participate in civic debates and never be afraid to run for office. I had no idea how rewarding public office could be. Having a vote and a voice in the most important national legislature on the globe and dealing with the most interesting cast of characters ever assembled is impossible to describe.

As I look back, I wish I could say my generation made everything perfect so your generation can take a sabbatical from civics and politics. I can't say that. I wrote a book titled *Twenty-four Years of House Work and the Place is Still a Mess*. The title sums it up. Because we are human, I do not think we will ever make things perfect, but I can say things are better in this country because many of us worked very hard on problems that seemed unsolvable. Hopefully you will pick up the torch. Keep chasing those who would defile the environment, derail democracy, roll back all the gains that generations of Americans have made, and hand off the torch to your children when they are ready. If you like people, you will love politics. Many want to say "poltics" means many blood sucking insects. It will mean that only if you defer and let others define your future. Grab the torch and go!

Patricia Schroeder, a Democrat from Colorado, was the longest-serving woman in the United States House of Representatives, having been reelected 11 times.

12 | Good Luck

P eople usually can answer the question: What kind of a world would you like for yourself, your children, and generations to come? That should be followed by another question: What are you willing to do to achieve it? When the second question is asked, people start their verbal stumbling. The fact that you have read this far indicates that either you have a demanding and good teacher, or you have at least a generalized feeling that in some way you should contribute to a better community and world. It may indicate both—a good teacher and a good attitude.

A good attitude is not simply having concern, but a positive outlook that recognizes there are problems, and that people of goodwill working on difficulties can improve things. If you have a negative attitude toward everything—and you know people like that—it is unlikely you will contribute much. Years ago a man staying at the Waldorf-Astoria Hotel in New York City, one of the finest hotels anywhere, called the manager to complain, "I paid big money for this suite and in the rooms next to mine a man keeps playing the piano and prevents me from taking a nap." The hotel manager replied that he sympathized with his guest but told him that the man playing the piano in the next suite was Ignacy Paderewski, then the world's most famous pianist. Upon hearing that the man called his friends and said with great enthusiasm, "Come to my suite at the Waldorf and you can listen to Paderewski practicing in the room next to mine!" What had changed? Had the piano playing changed? The facts were all the same, but the attitude had changed, and what seemed to be an unpleasant barrier to a good afternoon nap suddenly became the source of great pride.

The attitude with which you approach politics will make a huge difference in your enjoying it or not enjoying it, and between being effective or not being effective.

If you become a candidate or a campaign manager or someone who assists a candidate, you will experience the joy of winning or the sorrow of losing. But either of those momentary feelings will pass, and you will look back on your experience as a deeply enriching one.

Work hard.

Do what you believe to be right. Support the causes in which you genuinely believe. Be willing to risk votes by standing for causes that may not be popular.

Be creative.

On Election Day, remember that many of those who said they would vote for you probably will not. Be prepared emotionally to lose. If you do lose, place a phone call to the person who won to congratulate him or her—even if you do not feel like making that call. It is the "class" thing to do, and it helps to smooth the bumps in our democracy.

Also, be emotionally prepared to win. If you win, thank your supporters and be gracious to your opponent as well as to those who supported your opponent. It is the right thing to do—and it would be nice to have their support the next time you run.

If we could be there in person to shake your hand and wish you the best, we would. Now you will have to be satisfied with these last words of good wishes. You're going to see to it that our train of freedom and democracy keeps moving ahead, and we're proud of you for doing that.

Index

146